Athene Series
Feminist Scholarship on Culture and Education

Black Feminist Criticism
Perspectives on Black Women Writers
Barbara Christian

Narodniki Women
Russian Women Who Sacrificed Themselves for the Dream of Freedom
Margaret Maxwell

Speaking Freely
Unlearning the Lies of the Fathers' Tongues
Julia Penelope

The Reflowering of the Goddess
Gloria Feman Orenstein

Female-Friendly Science
Applying Women's Studies Methods and Theories to Attract Students
Sue V. Rosser

The Sexual Liberals and the Attack on Feminism
Dorchen Leidholdt &
Janice G. Raymond, Editors

Between Worlds
Women Writers of Chinese Ancestry
Amy Ling

Whence the Goddesses
A Source Book
Miriam Robbins Dexter

Made to Order
The Myth of Reproductive and Genetic Progress
Patricia Spallone &
Deborah Lynn Steinberg,
Editors

Exposing Nuclear Phallacies
Diana E. H. Russell, Editor

Teaching Science and Health from a Feminist Perspective
A Practical Guide
Sue V. Rosser

Taking Our Time
Feminist Perspectives on Temporality
Frieda Johles Forman &
Caoran Sowton, Editors

Educating for Peace
A Feminist Perspective
Birgit Brock-Utne

Men's Studies Modified
The Impact of Feminism on the Academic Disciplines
Dale Spender, Editor

Stopping Rape
Successful Survival Strategies
Pauline B. Bart &
Patricia H. O'Brien

Feminism Within the Science and Health Care Professions
Overcoming Resistance
Sue V. Rosser, Editor

Feminist Perspectives on Peace and Peace Education
Birgit Brock-Utne

Feminist Approaches to Science
Ruth Bleier, Editor

Science and Gender
A Critique of Biology and Its Theories on Women
Ruth Bleier

Women, Science, and Society

THE CRUCIAL UNION

Sue V. Rosser

Teachers College, Columbia University
New York and London

Published by Teachers College Press, 1234 Amsterdam Avenue, New York, NY 10027

An earlier version of Chapter 2 appeared under the title "The Next Millennium Is Here Now: Feminist Perspectives on Biotechnics and Reproductive Technologies," in *Transformations, 8* (1997).

Portions of Chapters 3, 4, and 5 are reprinted from *Women's Studies International Forum, 22,* Sue V. Rosser, "International Experiences Lead to Using Postcolonial Feminism to Transform Life Sciences Curriculum," pp. 3–15, copyright 1999, with permission from Elsevier Science.

Library of Congress Cataloging-in-Publication Data

Rosser, Sue Vilhauer.
    Women, science, and society : the crucial union / Sue V. Rosser.
      p.   cm.—(Athene series)
    Includes bibliographic references and index.
    ISBN 0-8077-3943-X (cloth : alk. paper). — ISBN 0-8077-3942-1 (pbk. : alk. paper)
    1. Women life scientists. 2. Women's studies. 3. Feminism. I. Title. II. Series.
QH305.5 .R67   2000
570'.82—dc21   99-086158

ISBN 0-8077-3942-1 (paper)
ISBN 0-8077-3943-X (cloth)

Printed on acid-free paper
Manufactured in the United States of America

07 06 05 04 03 02 01 00   8 7 6 5 4 3 2 1

For Pat

Contents

Acknowledgments

FORMAL RESEARCH, PAPERS, AND presentations, as well as informal conversations and suggestions of colleagues and students, stimulated, shaped, and influenced this book in overt and more subtle ways. I am particularly grateful to Banu Subramanian for allowing me to include "Snow Brown and the Seven Detergents: A Meta-narrative on Science and the Scientific Method" as the centerpiece for the conclusion. As she has done for four of my other books, Faye Chadwell developed an extensive bibliography of resources tailored to the topic of this volume, which provides readers with easier access to foundational and related sources. The opening quotes in Chapter 1 are drawn from Ambrose et al. (1997). The collaboration with Pat Miller and the analyses of graduate students Joann Benigno and Mireille Zieseniss formed the backbone for the case study of Chapter 1. The work of Marcia Good Maust for her master's thesis on caesarean section rates in Mexico, as well as conversations and presentations by her in the Gender and Science course she took with me, proved critical for the material in Chapter 2 regarding different feminist theoretical perspectives on cesarean sections. Anita Spring's research, particularly her Malawi book and her contributions to the Enset monograph, provided fundamental examples for Chapter 4. I am also grateful for her reading of that chapter and her invaluable additions, corrections, and suggestions for improvements.

I appreciate the comments and support from colleagues at the University of Florida and around the country who make my continuing work possible. Julie Montgomery and Paula Palmer from my office staff provided much-needed support on a daily basis, as they always do; Paula typed the references and reformatted the entire manuscript under severe time pressure. I am also most grateful to the editorial, production, copy-editing, and marketing staff at Teachers College Press. Without the energies and insights of Susan Liddicoat, Acquisitions Editor, who provided critical support at each step of the way, the book would not be here. As has been the situation with each of my books published by Teachers College Press, each member of the staff has been extremely professional, pleasant, and competent, which facilitates completion of the project.

Finally, I would like to thank my family, Pat, Caitlin, Meagan, Erica, and Kevin, as well as my mother, for their ongoing support of me and my work. Each of them contributed to the book in direct ways, such as reading a chapter or the entire manuscript or discussing a particular topic or point. Perhaps the indirect influences of learning their perspectives, their insights, and their varied approaches to life and the world taught me most of what I needed to write this volume. For that knowledge and their acceptance and love, I am very grateful.

The Confluence of Factors Demanding the Union of Women in the Life Sciences with Scholars in Women's Studies

GENETIC ENGINEERING, THE Human Genome Initiative (HGI), and indigenous medicines open new venues for interaction among countries and between genders. The large multinational corporations Monsanto and DuPont together now produce half of the soybean and more than half of the corn seed sold in the United States (King & Stabinsky, 1999). Using their life patents, they also have begun to license and patent germ plasmas from the seeds of the varieties of plants grown by women in developing countries. Patents on seeds provide a legal means to ensure that farmers buy seed every year, rather than seeding the next crop from the previous year's harvest. Pharmaceutical companies such as Merck have extracted and patented medicinal properties from plants and herbs known by women in indigenous cultures to have healing properties.

As these practices become more common, the potential for benefit for, or considerable harm to, women in developing countries increases. Introduction of genes for virus resistance or moisture retention might increase crop yields and food supplies, therefore allowing women to feed their families and ward off predicted famines. More likely, the companies may set the prices high enough that the women who initially held the seeds cannot buy the newly engineered strain. The shortage of food will become more acute, as developed countries use the new strain to produce higher yields per acre to sell on the world market. In a similar fashion, the newly patented extract from the medicinal plant may increase demand for the plant, thereby driving up its price and making it unavailable or very expensive for the people who have depended on its healing properties for generations.

The U.S. government, in response to pressures from corporations, has pressed hard for all countries to accept United States-style patent laws. The U.S. government threatened to end science and technology agreements with India unless the Indian patent laws were extended to cover pharmaceutical and agricultural products (King & Stabinsky, 1999). Ironically, the same laws and international agreements that make these patents possible to be used for genes and extracts from materials from developing countries also permit patenting of genes such as the BRCA1 and 2 breast cancer genes in the United States. Women in Southern and Northern continents may both suffer, although in different ways, from these technologies, patents, and agreements. With their scientific and medical knowledge, life scientists and physicians who also are feminists can work with researchers from other backgrounds in women's studies to ensure that the work, knowledge, and lives of women are preserved and enhanced, rather than destroyed.

During the last quarter of a century, groundbreaking work has occurred in biology, health, and women's studies. Characterized as cutting-edge, all three of these interdisciplinary areas have been marked as frontiers for the 2000s. Although the overlap between the research in biology and its applications in health has been explored and assumed, the intersection of women's studies with the life sciences has been examined much less.

A few scholars within women's studies have developed feminist critiques of science, but until recently the humanities and social sciences served as sources for most of the scholars and research in women's studies. Science has remained on the margins of women's studies; many women's studies programs have no scientists on their faculties. Women now receive almost half of the undergraduate and 45% of the graduate degrees in the life sciences (National Science Foundation, Division of Science Resource Studies, 1997a) and constitute 42% of medical student enrollments (Bickel, Croft, Johnson, & Marshall, 1997). Although women scientists may recognize on some level that the women's movement may have contributed generally to removal of quotas and encouragement for women to enter science, many remain unaware of, or uninterested in, women's studies and feminist critiques of science. In short, women scientists and women's studies scholars have developed along parallel paths, with little crossover between them. Although the life sciences and women's studies have contributed some of the most exciting research of the late 1990s, scholars in each field have not crossed the border to learn how work in the other can enhance their own work.

THREE SIGNIFICANT FACTORS

A unique confluence of factors demands that women scientists and scholars in women's studies now join together. The critical mass of women in the life sciences and medicine constitutes the first of these factors. A number of studies have explored why women during the past 2 decades have been attracted in large numbers to most of the life science disciplines, including molecular biology, plant physiology and pathology, and ecology, as well as zoology, botany, and medicine. An overwhelming reason given by women in most studies emerges from their desire to help people. Women are particularly attracted to science when they can see its relationship to life in general and most particularly when they see its usefulness in helping human beings. The life sciences, including medicine, clearly fit this parameter.

A second factor provides a particular opportunity for the increasing concentrations of women in the life sciences. During most of the twentieth century, the physical sciences, particularly physics, held the status of the preeminent field where the intellectual frontiers of science might yield the most fruitful research. Gradually, biology has come to occupy the place held by physics in mid-century. While remaining tight overall, resources for scientific research have shifted gradually from the physical sciences to the life sciences, with considerable increases in budgets of the National Institutes of Health and other agencies that fund biomedical and environmental research (Greenberg, 1999). These budget shifts indicate the intellectual shift in scientific thought that the life sciences are now perceived as the fertile field that will yield the fundamental, significant research results. Having larger numbers of women in the predominant frontier for research provides a fortuitous opportunity for women to shape the research agenda and its applications in the 2000s.

A third factor, women's studies, holds the potential to influence the interaction between research done in the life sciences and that in the humanities and social sciences. The burgeoning scholarship by scientists in women's studies, often initiated and enriched by their humanities colleagues in philosophy and history of science, has made gender and science one of the cutting-edge areas that will bring major contributions to feminism in the first decade of the 2000s.

The confluence of these three factors—critical mass of women in biology and medicine, the life sciences as the frontier for research in the next millennium, and the readiness of women's studies to place gender and science in central focus—provides a unique opportunity. Working together, scholars in women's studies, scientists, and physicians can use feminism to examine the frontiers of biotechnology and reproductive technologies. Without feminist lenses, women, society, and science may all suffer as the development and application of these technologies proceed and expand.

In the bibliography developed to accompany this volume, librarian Faye Chadwell points out particular articles, books, and Internet resources on feminism, science, women's health, women and development, and bio- and reproductive technologies. These serve as invaluable resources to initiate physicians, scientists, experts in international development, and women's studies scholars to the research in each other's fields with which they may be less familiar.

STAGES OF WOMEN'S STUDIES

This volume uses the stages through which women's studies is moving as a framework to examine how women—as scientists, feminists, consumers, policy makers, mothers, and global citizens—may affect and be affected by bio- and reproductive technologies.

Arising from the civil rights movement and the women's movement, women's studies began in the 1960s, with the first two programs established in 1969–70 (Hedges, 1997). Characterized as the stage of recovery of lost texts and figures, early work in women's studies recognized that traditional academic fields had failed to account for women's experiences, social actions, and contributions to culture. At this stage scholars used this realization as the basis to search for where and why women were missing from fields and how their absence had led to flaws, distortions, and biases in disciplinary research.

Within this framework, the first chapter of this volume examines statistics on women in science and medicine to understand the foundations of the current critical mass of women in the life sciences and medicine. This foundation makes it possible for women to have an impact on the research directions and applications in ways not open to women in the physical sciences because of their small numbers. It examines how women's differing interests, life experiences, and perspectives may lead them to ask new questions, take different approaches, and find alternative interpretations, leading to new theories and conclusions drawn from the data. Comparing men's and women's reasons for studying life sciences elucidates these differences.

In their eagerness to make women visible and defined as a category in traditional academic disciplines, many scholars in women's studies made a mistake that paralleled the error of which they accused their male colleagues. Just as women's studies scholars revealed that the assumption that male experience coincided with human experience constituted a form of androcentric bias that rendered women invisible, these same scholars mistakenly assumed that the experience of all women was the same. Women of color, working-class women, and lesbian women pointed out that their experiences as women did not fit the depictions of many women's studies scholars, which appeared to emanate from a White, middle-class, heterosexual perspective.

This revelation led to the recognition that gender did not represent a homogeneous category of analysis and that gender needed to be studied in relationship to other oppressions of race, class, nationalism, and sexual orientation. Multiple theories of feminism, ranging from liberal through socialist, womanist, essentialist, radical, and postcolonial feminism, emerged from this revelation. In Chapter 2 each of these theories reveals at least one, if not multiple, insights for how bio- and reproductive technologies might affect women from different backgrounds and in different situations. Taken together, they provide multifaceted perspectives from which to assess the development and implementation of these technologies.

As scholars began to explore the relationships among race, class, gender, and other factors, women's studies entered a stage in the 1980s that focused on the analysis of gender as a social category. During this phase, critics began to question the ways in which gender determines the structure of social organizations, systems of cultural production, and representations of sexuality. Exploration of this latter category led to an examination of the roles of masculinity and femininity and definitions of the history of sexualities. Women's studies scholars interested in science and medicine explored how the scientific and medical hierarchy both reflected and reinforced gender roles, including overt, covert, and subtle barriers and obstacles that maintained male dominance, status, and high salaries as removal of official quotas permitted women to enter the professions. Studies of the history of science revealed the roots of modern science in a mechanistic model in which objectivity became synonymous with masculinity and that encouraged the domination of male scientists over women, nature, and more holistic models of the world.

Simultaneously, scholars in humanities and social sciences developed postcolonial critiques to understand aspects of nationalism and globalization. These critiques revealed a stage in which Western/Northern countries ignored, underdeveloped, and wrote out of history the intellectual, artistic, and cultural contributions of civilizations located in Eastern/ Southern continents. Feminists turned these postcolonial critiques to an examination of the particular ways that women living in previously colonized countries had become invisible, exotic, or stereotyped in certain roles to Northerners. Chapter 3 uses postcolonial feminisms to explore how the contributions to science and technology of women from Southern continents might be initiated into Northern science education.

The exploration of gender as a social category and the separation of the roles of masculinity and femininity from the biological sexes of male and female provided invaluable insights for women's studies scholars working in all areas, including science and medicine. More recently, some poststructuralist and postmodern theorists have proposed that all is construct. With no objective reality, gender, class, and race all represent masks or identities that may be tried on, transgressed, and transformed. Some versions of these theories would suggest that science also represents a construct and that notions of reliability, verifiability, as well as objectivity are useless.

Although the science wars and difficulties with postmodernism will not constitute a major thread of this volume, they do provide a backdrop for Chapter 4. Extreme emphasis on gender, along with a failure to focus on women, has led to problems for applications of agricultural technologies in Africa. As biotechnologies and reproductive technologies reach further into Africa and other developing countries, their potential solutions to food shortages and population issues may be more problematic if they are explored in the context of the social construction of gender without attention to the material, daily lives of women. Life scientists who have developed and understand the research behind these techniques, as well as agricultural and health care workers who implement them, bring an immediacy to this debate based on their experiences as feminists working with women in developing countries.

During the past decade, women's studies in the United States has begun to recognize the influence of globalization and the significance of understanding international perspectives and movements. Much in the same way that early feminism suffered from the failure to recognize diversity among women in the United States with regard to race, class, sexual orientation, and other factors in its eagerness to discover the influence of gender, more recently scholars in women's studies have realized the constraints of not understanding the experiences of women in different countries and cultural contexts and their connections and relationships to women's lives in the United States.

International and global perspectives represent a stage in which scientists and health care professionals who are feminists can lead the way for other scholars in women's studies. Science traditionally has been defined as an international endeavor, and the scientific community has networks and experience in working on global problems across international boundaries. Work done by life scientists on agriculture with women in developing countries and by health professionals on international reproductive health rights and issues serves as groundbreaking work for the feminist analyses of biotechnologies and reproductive technologies. Chapter 4 explores how globalization and these technologies provide opportunities to enhance or destroy women's work and knowledge. With their scientific and medical knowledge, life scientists and physicians who also are feminists can work with researchers from other backgrounds in women's studies to ensure that the work and knowledge of women in developing countries are preserved and enhanced, rather than destroyed.

The science wars developing from postmodern theories and increasing globalization have drawn the attention of feminists to the necessity for the fusion of theory and practice, an issue that signals an emerging stage in women's studies. Since women's studies arose as the academic arm of an activist women's movement, many feminists have grown troubled by a tendency for postmodernism to lead to political inactivism. Although some postmodern feminists have attempted to explain the compatibility of these theories with political activity, the theories have created a schism. In some institutions, some feminists doing high theory have found women's studies scholars, particularly those in the social and natural sciences, as well as some other areas in the humanities, deficient in theory. Simultaneously, women's studies scholars have noted the absence of practice and grounding in the realities of women's lives in the work of the high theorists.

To survive as an interdisciplinary area embracing all feminists, women's studies must begin to fuse theory with practice. This serves as another stage where women's studies scholars, scientists, and health care professionals may provide significant contributions. Based in laboratory and clinical practice, the fusion of theory and practice is woven into the fabric of the life sciences and medicine. Although much of the mainstream of biology and medicine has remained untouched by critiques of objectivity, feminists in these areas have had to grapple with the issue and have developed some limited parameters to mediate between the construct of science and the reliable and verifiable data that are crucial to the field. Chapter 5 examines the fusion between theory and practice of science, using the lens of postcolonial theory to explore the effects of bio- and reproductive technologies on the lives of women in three different cultures on three continents. The similar, but locally transformed, ways these technologies affect U.S. women's lives drive home the need for activism in the context of global theory and the lives of immigrant women scientists in North America.

The book concludes with personal revelations from a woman scientist shaped by her postcolonial experiences and a response by the author.

This constitutes a call for women to come together to shape the research agenda for biotechnologies and reproductive technologies and to guide their implementation in ways to help, rather than hurt, all women. Without the perspectives of feminist scientists who have developed and understood these technologies, feminist physicians who work with women using reproductive technologies, and feminist scholars in women's studies who study women's lives and experiences in diverse global and local cultures, all women may suffer. By uniting our talents and perspectives, we can save science, other women who do not have the professional expertise to guide this research and its implementation, and ultimately ourselves.

Critical Mass: Women Life Scientists and Physicians

I am a physician. I am concerned with the health and welfare of people. Even as a little girl, when I was chopping cotton all day in a field in Arkansas, getting an education to help people was a great dream, even though it seemed impossible, even though becoming a physician was then beyond my wildest dreams. . . . Every week I see children who are my patients in the endocrinology clinic at Arkansas Children's Hospital. Many of them are children of poor families. Having been a Black child from a poor rural family in Arkansas, I identify strongly with them. It is important to me that each person is treated with the same dignity and deference as a multimillionaire. . . . As long as there is one child who is not cared for properly, nurtured lovingly, educated wisely, or one teen who commits suicide; as long as there is one adult who is without health care, without friends, without community; as long as there is one elderly person without medical care, without shelter and food, we cannot stop working to raise consciousness. Somehow, in spite of great improbabilities, I find myself in a position to speak for the people who are not forgotten, and I will never stop.

—M. Joycelyn Elders, Professor of Pediatrics, University of Arkansas School for Medical Sciences

I've always liked science and working with people. I don't know exactly when those impulses began coming together as an interest in medicine, but it was sometime in high school. There aren't any doctors in my family, so I didn't really have any role models, but medicine seemed like a way to accommodate my combined interest in science and medicine. . . . There was a clear need to take better care of women with breast problems, and I realized that I could help in a way that a lot of people couldn't; so I decided to specialize.

—Susan Love, Director, Revlon/UCLA Breast Center, University of California at Los Angeles

I'm a physician epidemiologist, but I identify most with being a pediatrician. . . . I became interested in HIV/AIDS research very early in the epidemic and very early in my career. In 1982, when I was a pediatric intern at the Children's Hospital in Boston, I saw children who appeared to have an acquired immunodeficiency that was new, the cause of which wasn't known. We knew they were very sick and that they invariably died, but we could only give them supportive care. It wasn't until 1983 that the HIV virus was discovered as the underlying cause of their illness. . . . My goal for the future is to continue population-based research that will improve the health of the American people.

—Evelyn M. Rodriguez, Associate Director for Research and Senior Medical Officer, Bureau of Health Resources Development, Department of Health and Human Services

As I was growing up, I saw the destruction of the Shuswap Lake area. Houses were built in all the special places I used to go. I saw a bulldozer rip down the cliffs where calypso orchids grew. I saw nature losing out, and it became a fundamental issue for me. Also, the people of the First Nations that I knew while growing up were being treated very poorly. They had a low view of themselves. My grandparents were homesteaders and would never have survived without the help of the Salish in the Squamish Valley. I knew the Salish to be clever, helpful people; but just like the natural habitats that I loved, they were losing out. I became interested in what happens to people of the First Nations when their culture clashes with newer populations. These experiences influenced what I studied and the job I eventually took. They also influenced my drive to do science.

—Sonja Teraguchi, Curator of Invertebrate Zoology, Cleveland Museum of Natural History

I identify research topics in three ways: things that I know and know how to do, things that are intellectually exciting and challenging, and problems that are significant in terms of their severity or pervasiveness of impact. My current research involves two major projects: one in environmental exposure and infectious disease, conducted primarily in Brazil; the other on endocrine disruption, where I'm looking into chemicals like dioxin that affect reproduction and development.

—Ellen Kovner Silbergeld, Professor, University of Maryland Medical School

THE PROBLEM OF THE low numbers of women in science, mathematics, engineering, and technology continues to dominate news media and lead to funding for special programs to attract and retain women in these fields. Closer examination of the data reveals considerable variation among disciplines in the percentages of women. In some areas, such as engineering, physics, and computer sciences, the percentages of women receiving degrees were below 20% in 1996 (NSF, 1997a). In contrast, the biological/agricultural sciences now award women half of the field's undergraduate degrees and almost 40% of the Ph.D.s. These percentages of degree recipients translate slowly into increases of women in the workforce, since the bulk of the workforce consists of individuals who received their degrees more than 10 years ago. As the report, "A Study on the Status of Women Faculty in Science at MIT," demonstrates, discrimination prevents women from reaching tenure and the ranks of professor and department head with comparable frequency relative to their male counterparts and that treatment worsens as women's careers progress (Miller & Wilson, 1999).

Yet, as the latest data reveal (NSF, 1997a), despite their dearth in engineering, physics, and computer sciences, women have reached a critical mass in several areas, including the life sciences, social sciences, and medicine. Equally important, studies, some of which will be considered later in this chapter, document that women are especially attracted to science for its practical applications and social usefulness, particularly in helping people.

In contrast, the equipment-oriented, hardware-intensive disciplines, such as physics, computer and information sciences, and mechanical and electrical engineering, represent the areas with fewest women. Pursuing that path even further, I suggest that it is the most people-oriented or patient-intensive specialties in medicine—primary care, pediatrics, and psychiatry—that contain the most women. The quotations from prominent women physicians and scientists that began this chapter exemplify the reasons women give for choosing these professions. Because of their common backgrounds, interest in helping people, and commitment to women, scientists, physicians, and scholars in women's studies can make a difference in bio- and reproductive technologies by working together now.

STATISTICAL BACKGROUND FOR THE CRITICAL MASS

Three decades ago the percentages of women receiving graduate degrees in science, engineering, and mathematics and of women receiving M.D.s both hovered in the single digits. In 1965, women constituted 6.8% of the graduates of U.S. medical schools (Bickel, Croft, Johnson, & Marshall, 1997, Table 1), and in 1966, they constituted 8.0% of the Ph.D. recipients

Table 1.1. Women Medical School Applicants, Enrollees, and Graduates, Selected Years, 1949–50 Through 1997–98

	Applicants		New Entrants		Total Enrolled		Graduates	
	No.	%	No.	%	No.	%	No.	%
1949–50	1,390	5.7	387	5.5	1,806	7.2	595	10.7
1959–60	1,026	6.9	494	6.0	1,710	5.7	405	5.7
1964–65	1,731	9.0	786	8.9	2,503	7.7	503	6.8
1969–70	2,289	9.4	929	9.1	3,390	9.0	700	8.4
1974–75	8,712	20.4	3,263	22.4	9,661	18.0	1,706	13.4
1979–80	10,222	28.3	4,575	27.8	16,141	25.3	3,497	23.1
1984–85	12,476	34.7	5,469	33.4	21,316	31.8	4,632	28.3
1985–86	11,562	35.2	5,520	33.9	21,650	32.5	4,904	30.1
1986–87	11,267	36.0	5,574	34.6	22,100	33.4	4,957	30.8
1987–88	10,411	37.0	5,767	36.2	22,544	34.3	5,107	32.3
1988–89	10,264	38.4	5,878	36.8	22,985	35.2	5,215	32.8
1989–90	10,546	39.2	6,025	38.0	23,513	36.2	5,221	33.4
1990–91	11,785	40.3	6,153	38.5	24,286	37.3	5,231	34.0
1991–92	13,700	41.1	6,433	39.7	24,962	38.1	5,553	36.0
1992–93	15,619	41.8	6,772	41.6	26,038	39.4	5,550	36.1
1993–94	17,957	42.0	6,851	42.0	26,854	40.3	5,880	38.0
1994–95	18,968	41.8	6,819	41.9	27,552	41.1	5,919	38.1
1995–96	19,779	42.5	6,941	42.7	28,031	41.9	6,232	39.2
1996–97	20,031	42.6	6,917	42.7	28,404	42.2	6,509	40.9
1997–98 (est.)	18,196	42.5						

Reprinted, by permission, from J. Bickel, K. Croft, D. Johnson, & R. Marshall, *Women in U.S. Academic Medicine: Statistics 1997* (Washington, D.C.: Association of American Medical Colleges, 1997).

in all fields of science, engineering, and mathematics, including the social sciences (NSF, 1997b, p. 82). As these data suggest, the percentage of women in medical school was actually lower than that of women in science, engineering, and mathematics graduate school, although some might argue that the inclusion of social sciences raised the percentage of women in the NSF data in ways that make those data less comparable to the medical school statistics. Comparison of the data for M.D. recipients (Table 1.1) and Ph.D. recipients in science, engineering, and mathematics (Figure 1.1) shows that by 1996, the most recent year for which comparable data are available, the percentage of women receiving M.D.s (39.2%) (Bickel et al., 1997, Table 1) surpassed that of women receiving Ph.D.s in science, engineering, and mathematics (31.8%) (NSF, 1997b, p. 12), even with the inclusion of the social sciences.

In 1996, the percentage of women receiving master's degrees in science, engineering, and mathematics (39.0%; see Figure 1.2) virtually equaled that for women receiving M.D.s (39.2%; refer back to Table 1.1).

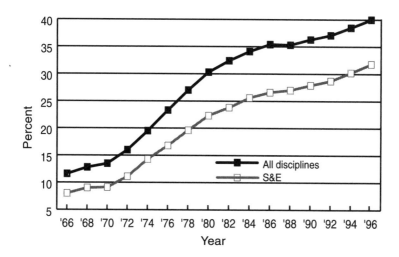

Figure 1.1. Doctorates awarded to women as percentage of all doctorates and as percentage of all science and engineering (S & E) doctorates, 1966–1996. The S & E category includes mathematics and corresponds to the science, engineering, and mathematics category discussed in the text. All figures courtesy National Science Foundation, Science Resources Studies Division.

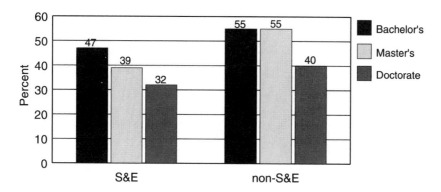

Figure 1.2. Percentages of bachelor's, master's, and doctoral degrees in S & E and in all fields awarded to women, 1996.

In contrast, in 1966, the percentage of women receiving M.S.s (13.3%) in science, engineering, and mathematics (NSF, 1997a, p. 81) had been considerably higher than the percentage receiving M.D.s (6.8%) (Bickel et al., 1997, Table 1). Although few would argue that an M.S. ranks as high as an M.D. by academic criteria, I include the data from the M.S. recipients, since the academic standing of the M.D. appears to lie somewhere between the M.S. and the Ph.D. Universities normally consider the Ph.D. to constitute the highest degree of rank, since it requires original research and the writing of a dissertation in addition to course work. The M.D., a professional degree, ranks lower by these academic criteria. M.D./Ph.D. programs provide a route for physicians planning a research career to receive the research/thesis training necessary for a Ph.D., while recognizing that much of the coursework for a M.D. may fulfill Ph.D. course requirements.

A closer look at the data reveals considerable disparities among the various science, engineering, and mathematics disciplines in the percentages of women receiving graduate degrees, from lows in engineering to highs in psychology. Excluding engineering, which overall has maintained rock bottom percentages of women for decades (a particularly unfortunate trend, since the overall engineering workforce is larger by almost one-third than the overall science workforce), the percentage of women varies considerably among the other disciplines, as shown in Figure 1.3. Com-

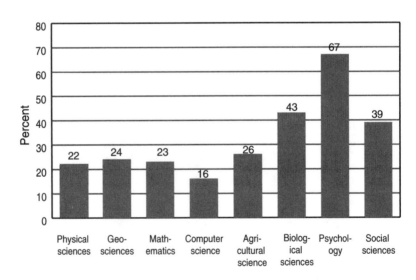

Figure 1.3. Percentages of doctoral degrees in sciences awarded to women, 1996.

puter science represents not only the broadly categorized field with the lowest percentage of women, but it also represents the only field in which the percentage of women decreased, from 21.9% to 16% between 1985 and 1996 (NSF, 1997b). The relative standing among the other broad categories remained approximately the same, and the percentages of women Ph.D. recipients increased (NSF, 1997b).

Considerable variation also exists among the subdisciplines within each broad category. Within the physical sciences, in 1996 the range of women receiving Ph.D.s ran from a high of 28.2% in chemistry through 21.4% in astronomy to a low of 13.0% in physics. Within earth, atmospheric, and ocean sciences (identified as geosciences in the figure), the range spanned 29.1% in oceanography through 19.5% in geosciences to 17.6% in atmospheric sciences. Within mathematical sciences, more women received Ph.D.s in mathematics (23%) than in computer sciences (16%).

Engineering has a smaller percentage of women Ph.D.s than any other broad category within the sciences. Figure 1.4 shows selected data from 1996, when some subdisciplines within engineering, such as biomedical (22.3%; not shown), industrial (15%), metallurgical/materials (19%),

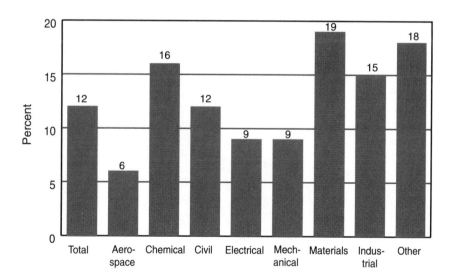

Figure 1.4. Percentages of doctoral degrees in engineering awarded to women, 1996.

chemical (16%), and agricultural (16.3%; not shown), engineering surpassed the percentages of women in physics (13.0%) (NSF, 1997b). The smallest percentages of women clustered in mining (9.7%; not shown), aeronautical/astronautical (6%), mechanical (9%), and petroleum engineering (5.8%; not shown). Civil engineering (12%), nuclear engineering (8.0%; not shown), engineering science (7.7%; not shown), and electrical engineering (9%) also attracted low numbers of women (NSF, 1997b).

Among the social sciences, higher percentages of women occur in general, although wide variances exist among the disciplines. Psychology has by far the largest numbers of women, with 66.7% of Ph.D.s going to women (refer back to Figure 1.3). The other eight subdisciplines shown in Figure 1.5 rank as follows with regard to women: anthropology (56%), sociology (56%), linguistics (56%), area and ethnic studies (50%), history and philosophy of science (38%), political science (30%), and economics (23%) with "other social sciences" accounting for 46%.

The subdisciplinary breakdown proves useful in tearing apart the discrepant percentages between women in science, engineering, and mathematics graduate school and medicine. The majority of students enrolling in medical school come from undergraduate majors in the biological sciences or chemistry. Separating the data from the other science, engineering, and mathematics disciplines from the data from biology and

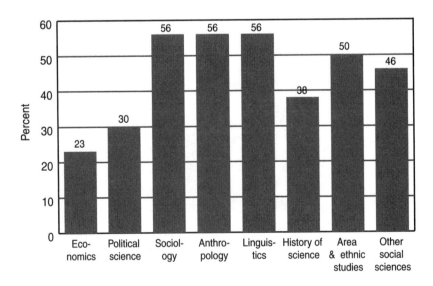

Figure 1.5. Percentages of doctoral degrees in social sciences awarded to women, 1996.

chemistry reveals that by 1995 women received 52.6% of the degrees in biological sciences. In chemistry women earned 42.3% of the bachelor's degrees in 1995. Comparisons for graduate enrollment reveal that in 1995, 52.0% of biological sciences master's degree recipients were women (NSF, 1997a, Table 49); in 1995 women constituted 42.0% of chemistry master's degree recipients (NSF, 1997a, Table 37). In 1995, women received 42.2% of the Ph.D.s in biological sciences; the percentages of women Ph.D.s in chemistry for the year totaled 30.6%.

These data suggest that the percentages of women in those graduate science, engineering, and mathematics fields that more closely parallel the sciences of medical school compare very favorably with the 38.1% of women graduating from medical school in 1994–95. These also represent the graduate science, engineering, and mathematics fields that draw from similar undergraduate majors held by the majority of medical students.

What meanings and implications can be inferred from these data demonstrating large numbers of women entering the medical profession and areas of science such as biology, chemistry, and other life sciences over the past 3 decades, while relatively fewer women have entered the physical sciences and engineering? What attracts women to medicine, health, and the life sciences? What impact will large numbers of women have on these fields in general and on the development and use of biological and reproductive technologies in women's lives in particular?

GENDER DIFFERENCES IN CAREER CHOICES
IN SCIENCE AND HEALTH FIELDS

Having spent much of my academic career studying women in science and women's health, I know of considerable scholarship on gender and science from studies undertaken at a variety of levels, for diverse purposes, and with somewhat different populations. This scholarship has explored gender differences in interests in science and in those who become particularly attracted to some fields in science and less attracted to others.

In her explorations of the reasons why women remain underrepresented in many high-status occupational fields, especially those associated with physical science, engineering, and applied mathematics, despite considerable recent efforts to increase their participation in those fields, Eccles (1994) and her colleagues (Eccles, 1987; Eccles & Harold, 1992; Jozefowicz, Barber, & Eccles, 1993) have examined some of the factors significant in career choices and achievement goals. In sum, their numerous studies on gifted students, coupled with those of others (Benbow & Stanley, 1984), reveal that females tend to be less confident of success than males in science-related professions, and males are less confident of their success than females in health-related professions, even those that involve extensive scientific training (Eccles, Barber, & Jozefowicz, 1997). When asked their occupational interests and/or anticipated college major, gifted girls rated biological science, and both medical and social service occupations and training, higher than the boys, while boys expressed more interest in both higher-status and business-related occupations in general, and in the physical sciences, engineering, and the military in particular (Benbow & Stanley, 1984; Fox, Pasternak, & Peiser, 1976). Females desired jobs that were people-oriented, while males placed a higher interest in jobs that allowed for work with machinery, math, or computers. Both wanted jobs that allowed flexibility to meet family obligations, entailed prestige and responsibility, and allowed for creative and intellectual work (Eccles, 1997).

Eccles (1997) also reports gender differences with regard to health and science/math careers. Both females and males who aspire to health careers expect to do well in health-related occupations and value people/society-oriented job characteristics. Only the females who aspire to health careers also expect to do well in science-related occupations; the males do not expect to do well in science-related occupations.

This work also uncovers differences between females who choose health in contrast to science/math careers. Both males and females who aspired to science/math careers expected to do well in science-related fields and valued math and computer job tasks when compared with others. Both males and females who chose science-related careers did not value people/society-oriented job characteristics. As Eccles (1997) concludes:

> Considering the fact that they both expect to do well in science-related careers, it follows that one of the critical components influencing females' decisions to go into a science vs. a health related field is not science-related efficacy but the value these females place on having a job associated with people and humanistic concerns. Thus, increased emphasis on the humanistic and people-oriented aspects of science-related careers, not increased emphasis on ability perceptions alone, is important in encouraging more females to consider science-related occupations. (p. 16)

Eccles and her colleagues built on the work of Boswell (1979), showing that both boys and girls stereotype mathematicians and scientists as loners who have little time for their families or friends because they work long hours in a laboratory on abstract problems that typically have limited immediate social implications. They documented that female high school seniors placed more value than males on the importance of making occupational sacrifices for one's family and on the importance of having a job that allows one to help others and do something worthwhile for society. These data also revealed that gifted women desired a more varied, or multifaceted, type of life than men (at this age, at least). Coupling this with the work of Maines (1983), showing that women seem more likely than men to be involved in, and to value, competence in several activities simultaneously, may suggest why scientifically competent women are especially interested in biology, chemistry, medicine, and health, rather than physics, computer sciences, and engineering, which may have a narrower focus as well as lacking orientation toward people.

Other studies provide supporting evidence that helping others and doing something worthwhile for society serve as powerful motivators to attract women to science in general, and to the biosciences and health in particular. Astin and Sax (1996), in their studies of majors of first-year college students, document that students who switch from physical science majors to other sciences tend to choose biology. This trend holds particularly true for females, with 7.8% of the final women majors (5.8% of final men majors) in biological sciences coming from the physical sciences (Astin & Sax, 1996, p. 104). Rarely do these women switch because of problems with grades or achievement in the physical sciences; more typically they become restive with the absence of people orientation and/or because of their attraction to other fields. In addition to biology, women leaving physical science majors switched to psychology, education, and the humanities, while men leaving switched to the social sciences and business.

The studies of Seymour and Hewitt (1994) also suggest gender differences in why people switch majors. The college women gave "non-SME major offers interest" as the most frequent (46.2%) reason for switching; college men ranked that as fifth (27%), with "lack of/loss of interest in SME: 'turned off science'" as the most frequent (43.8%), which women ranked as their second most frequent reason (43.0%) for switching. As suggested in the Astin and Sax (1996) data, the Seymour and Hewitt (1994) studies also reveal that women leave science because of their service orientation to help others in difficulty; understanding how science helps people also may retain women:

> Altruistic reasons for choosing SME majors are predominantly expressed (90.9%) by women and students of color. . . . Women are more likely than men to rank materialistic goals below the desire to do something they care about, either as a matter of personal fulfillment, or in pursuit of a valued social cause. (p. 103)

A CASE STUDY

Aware of these data documenting gender differences in choices among the science disciplines, the particular interest of women attracted to science in non-SME areas, and the draw of women to science when they perceive its usefulness in helping people, we (Miller, Rosser, Benigno, & Zieseniss, in press) decided to examine some of these factors more closely in a selected group of college juniors and seniors. We chose a group of re- search-oriented, highly motivated students with strong academic records in the sciences, to ensure that having difficulty with science courses or a lack of interest in research could not be factors.

The sample was the 120 most recent (1992–97) Interdisciplinary Stud- ies Majors (IDS) in the College of Liberal Arts and Sciences at the Univer- sity of Florida in biochemistry and neurobiology, the two main science tracks. We compared various aspects of the IDS applications of the most recent 30 male and 30 female graduates in each of the two tracks. We were particularly interested in gender differences in their "personal statements" (reasons for pursuing the major and plans for the future).

The research-oriented IDS program is limited to academically accom- plished juniors and seniors, with a minimum GPA of 3.0, a B; the majority graduate with honors. Students apply after taking certain basic science courses required for each major. Students must be highly motivated to enter these science majors because the application process requires consid- erable time. The application consists of letters of recommendation from their faculty research supervisor and another faculty member from a different department, a proposal describing their research project that will lead to a substantial senior thesis, a list of proposed core and elective courses, and a statement describing their career plans and reasons for choice of the major. Most enter medical school, Ph.D. programs in science, or both. At the time of application (usually junior year), students already are working in a laboratory or soon will be. They typically conduct re- search for 1 to 2 years as undergraduates.

Analyses of the data using chi-square tests uncovered no significant gender differences with regard to GPA, core and elective courses, or major at the time of application. Similarly, analyses of personal statements revealed no gender differences in students' desires for a Ph.D. and a career in teaching or research, or in their pursuing the IDS major because it permitted them to combine interests, was more challenging, permitted greater depth of study, or allowed a wider range of courses.

Desire to pursue an M.D./Ph.D. stood out as the one career objective given by males much more frequently than females. More females than males majoring in either neurobiology or biochemistry wished to pursue an M.D.; almost three times as many women as men sought research experience. Qualitative analyses of the personal statements revealed significant differences in some career goals and interests. The most interesting outcome was that more than twice as many women as men gave what we termed "pro-social" reasons for their choices.

Miller and colleagues (in press) reported the following types of pro-social comments given by the women (the speaker's proposed major is given in brackets):

"Interaction with people" [neurobiology]

"I intend to spend two years in Thailand assisting in medical aid there." [neurobiology]

"Pursue a career which can provide medical care for others; research through which a multitude of people can be helped" [neurobiology]

"Serving in the Peace Corps" [biochemistry]

"I would love to participate in a cure for this deadly disease [cancer]." [biochemistry]

"I will pursue, as part of my career, learning the applications of biochemistry, physics, and other sciences relevant to the body with full interest in the subject matter and concern for the possibilities in helping others with this knowledge." [biochemistry]

"My ultimate goal is to establish a clinic in India to provide medical attention to the poor, starving citizens." [biochemistry]

"It will expose me to the many options in the field of medical research which will aid my practice as well as the community." [biochemistry]

Miller and colleagues (in press) categorized several comments made by men as pro-social. For the most part, those comments tended to focus more on contributions to knowledge or the discipline, than on serving/helping people directly:

"Perform EMG and kinematic studies to determine more beneficial physical therapies for people"

"Maybe in the process I will be able to configure a treatment to properly handle FAS [fetal alcohol syndrome] in children born of chronic alcoholic moms." [neurobiology]

"Background . . . will help me make a lasting contribution in the understanding of human behavior" [neurobiology]

"Expect to make an actual contribution as an undergrad" [neurobiology]

"Ultimately, I would like to head an environmental firm or organization, while educating the public on environmental issues." [biochemistry]

Contrasting the following complete paragraphs, the first written by a male student, ranked as pro-social, the second by a female student, places these phrases in the overall context. Both proposed neurobiology students wrote their responses to the question: "Give a brief statement of overall objectives of your proposed program. Concentrate on your goals for the first five–ten years after you graduate."

"Within the first five to ten years after I graduate, I hope to complete my graduate education with either an M.D. or a Ph.D. I aspire to become a pediatric neurologist or a neurodevelopmental disease researcher. The most ideal scenario would be if I could be both: having a practice as well as subjects for clinical research with cerebral palsy, Down's syndrome, and various other genetic neurodevelopmental diseases such as Batten's. I would hope that in some way, I will have furthered the knowledge within my field." [male] (in Miller et al., in press)

"I plan on continuing my education by entering medical school and pursuing a career where I can provide medical care for others. I would like to concentrate in the field of neurology not only through the treatment of disorders, but also through research of the subject. Due to my exposure to research, I realize research is a significant component of medical science. It is a way through which a multitude of people can be helped and great advancements can be made. I would like to pursue a career in both clinical work and research. I believe the proposed program would provide me with a balance of an intense curriculum and research experiences which will help me in my future medical career and enable my pursuit of scientific knowledge." [female] (in Miller et al., in press)

Both students have almost identical career goals of clinical and research practices. Both want to pursue scientific knowledge and contribute to the field. Although the line of research chosen by the man implies that it is likely to help others, the woman articulates her desire to help "a multitude of people."

The results of this study fall within the rubric of the many studies (Ambrose, Dunkle, Lazarus, Nair, & Harkus, 1997; Rosser, 1990) demonstrating that women enter science and health to help people. Working with people to save lives, improve their health, develop food and natural resources, and improve their quality of life becomes a powerful incentive for women to hone their scientific and technical skills.

These results, coupled with the studies documenting that women attracted to science also have interest in the humanities and social sciences, suggest that women scientists and physicians, more than their male counterparts, may be eager and open to learn from scholars in other disciplines, including ethics and women's studies, about the implications of the globalization of bio- and reproductive technologies on women's lives. Similarly, science and health have become the newest areas of development and expansion in women's studies research and teaching; these areas follow recent projects, still incomplete, to incorporate critical race theory and internationalization into women's studies curriculum. Current interest in media images and popular cultural portrayals of technology, the body, and science and medicine also have stimulated humanities scholars' desire to understand the basic research in science and technology underpinning these images and portrayals. Bio- and reproductive technologies stand as interdisciplinary intersections in women's lives on the two-way streets that connect the communities of humanities and social science scholars in women's studies, workers in women and development projects, scientists, and physicians.

Feminist Theoretical Perspectives:
Lenses on Bio- and Reproductive Technologies

PERHAPS IT IS NOT too surprising that biology is the area within the natural and physical sciences that has experienced the most interaction with women's studies and feminist critiques. Although biology of women and women's health courses have been taught for more than 2 decades at many U.S. universities, only within recent years have conferences and research agendas in the sciences begun to integrate women's studies and feminist perspectives. The Office of Women's Health Initiatives was established by the National Institutes of Health in 1991 (Pinn & LaRosa, 1992), but women's health curricula are just now making their way into mainstream medical schools and specialty requirements. In May 1996, I attended a Feminist Critique of the Human Genome Initiative conference funded by the Ethical Legal and Social Implications (ELSI) part of the $3 billion Human Genome Initiative; seeds for development of curricula that would focus on women's perspectives or critiques of the HGI were planted in the minds of various conference attendees. Between 1996 and 1999, while at the University of Florida, I became involved with WorldWID, a gender and development project that sharpened my knowledge of the impact of genetic engineering technologies on the lives of women in developing countries in Southern continents. I would like to explore the possibility of integration of gender into science and technology by looking at how feminisms, or, more accurately, different feminist theories, provide us with lenses to open new perspectives and provide insights into new ways of looking at research in biology and women's health and their respective applications in biotechnology and reproductive technologies.

In previous work (Rosser, 1994, 1995, 1997a, 1997b) I have explored interdisciplinary intersections and written about what can be learned from applying feminist theories to both education and research in women in science and women's health. While carefully discussing various theories, including liberal, Marxist/socialist, African American ethnic/womanist, essentialist, existentialist, psychoanalytic, radical, lesbian separatist, and postmodern feminism, I always omitted postcolonial feminism from the discussion until this book. Although the burgeoning scholarship (Achebe, 1988; Ashcroft, Griffiths, & Tiffin, 1995; Mohanty, 1984; Said, 1978; Spivak, 1988) on postcolonialism in general, and its feminist critiques in particular (Mohanty, 1984; Spivak, 1985; Suleri, 1992), had piqued my interest, I assumed it had little to do with my scholarship focus on pragmatic applications of feminist theories to issues surrounding curriculum, pedagogy, and research agendas for women and girls in science and health in the United States.

I recognized the United States as a colonizer of Mexico, Puerto Rico, Guam, the Virgin Islands, and other areas, and as a country very much involved in neocolonial enterprises such as economic and resource exploitation of so-called "developing" countries. However, since the United States has neither recently experienced colonization nor served as the colonizer in the same way that people living in countries from which the postcolonial critiques originated have experienced it, I incorrectly assumed that postcolonial feminist critiques had little or nothing to say directly regarding practical applications for science education and research agendas for the United States itself.

Although disciplines in the humanities and social sciences have employed postcolonial critiques for fruitful explorations of literature, culture, and social interactions, only recently have the philosophers of science (Haraway, 1989, 1992, 1997; Harding, 1993) begun to apply postcolonial critiques to the natural and physical sciences. Originally their applications focused on theoretical and language issues, rather than on practical implications for research agendas, education, and the workforce. Sandra Harding's most recent book, *Is Science Multicultural?* (1998), documents impacts and practical applications of de-development of Southern continents and conscious ignoring of indigenous women's science and technologies.

Postcolonial feminism will serve as the primary theoretical framework underpinning the subsequent chapters in this book. Later in this chapter I provide a definition of postcolonial feminism and briefly sketch some of the insights it provided for me into biology, health, and bio- and reproductive technologies.

Postcolonial feminist critiques emerged more recently in response to critiques of gaps in other feminist theories in women's studies and feminist literature, as well as in my own intellectual development. In this respect it follows the pattern of the increasing breadth, depth, and complexity of theories that posit gender as a central characteristic that interacts with other characteristics such as race and class, to structure relationships between individuals within groups, cultures, nations, and globally. Each theory arises both by building on the foundation of understanding laid by previous feminist theories and by identifying a failure to account for experiences, lives, or worldviews of significance omitted from earlier theories.

To provide the background, previous theories, and perspectives that led me to the definition of postcolonial feminist theory and insights into bio- and reproductive technologies used in this volume, I will discuss briefly several other feminist theories and the insights they gave me into these technologies. Because I have defined these theories in previous writings, I will only sketch a minimal definition for each theory here and proceed directly to my ideas regarding its implications for the technologies. For readers unfamiliar with my earlier work on these theories or for whom the definitions here appear incomplete or seem to rely on assumptions for which the implications are not well spelled out, or who want further background, please consult Chapter 5 of *Re-Engineering Female Friendly Science* (Rosser, 1997a) or Chapter 8 of *Women's Health: Missing from U.S. Medicine* (Rosser, 1994).

The variety and complexity of these various feminist theories provide a framework through which to explore research agendas in biology, health, biotechnology, and reproductive technologies. I will use these different feminist theories to examine the questions each would raise in specific applications to areas of research in biology and health. For the applications in biology, I speculate based on examples drawn from the Human Genome Initiative and genetic engineering of agricultural species; for health, the reproductive technologies of cesarean births, amniocentesis, and in vitro fertilization (IVF) serve as sources to initiate speculation. For each theory, I attempt to link global applications with local U.S. impacts.

LIBERAL FEMINISM

A general definition of liberal feminism is the belief that women are suppressed in contemporary society because they suffer unjust discrimination (Jaggar, 1983). Liberal feminists seek no special privileges for women and simply demand that everyone receive equal consideration without discrimination on the basis of sex.

Most scientists assume that the implications of liberal feminism extend only to employment, access, and discrimination issues. Their liberal-feminist focus revolves solely around removal of documented overt and covert barriers (Matyas & Malcom, 1991; NSF, 1992; Rosser, 1990; Rossiter,

1984, 1995; Vetter, 1988, 1992, 1996) that have prevented women from entering and succeeding in science.

Beyond this, liberal feminism accepts positivism as the theory of knowledge and assumes that human beings are highly individualistic and obtain knowledge in a rational manner that may be separated from their social conditions. Positivism implies that "all knowledge is constructed by inference from immediate sensory experiences" (Jaggar, 1983, pp. 355–356).

These assumptions lead to the belief in the possibilities of obtaining knowledge that is both objective and value-free, concepts that form the cornerstones of the scientific method. Objectivity is contingent upon value neutrality or freedom from values, interests, and emotions associated with a particular class, race, or gender. Liberal feminism also implies that the proportional representation of women in the scientific workforce will be achieved without changes in science itself, except for the removal of barriers.

In the past 2 decades feminist historians and philosophers of science (Fee, 1982; Haraway, 1989; Harding, 1986) and feminist scientists (Birke, 1986; Bleier, 1984, 1986; Fausto-Sterling, 1992; Hubbard, 1990; Keller, 1983, 1985; Rosser, 1988; Spanier, 1982) have pointed out a source of bias and absence of value neutrality in science, particularly biology. Experimental results in several areas in biology have been demonstrated to be biased or flawed because the experiments excluded females as subjects, focused on problems of primary interest to males, employed faulty designs, or interpreted data based on language or ideas constricted by patriarchal parameters.

Liberal feminism also does not question the integrity of the scientific method itself or of its supporting corollaries of objectivity and value neutrality. Liberal feminism reaffirms the idea that it is possible to find a perspective from which to observe that is truly impartial, rational, and detached. Lack of objectivity and presence of bias occur because of human failure properly to follow the scientific method and avoid bias due to situation or condition. Liberal feminists argue that it was through attempts to become more value-neutral that the possible androcentrism in previous scientific research was revealed.

Feminists have revealed a source of bias in many double-blind studies that were run using only male rats, human beings, or other primates as experimental subjects. In a double-blind study, neither the researcher nor the subjects know who among the subjects receives the true drug and who receives the placebo. This method is thought to ensure objectivity since neither party is biased by knowing who receives the drug. Perhaps the notion that the double-blind study ensures objectivity made the researchers overly confident of their results. In many cases (Steering Committee of the Physician's Health Study Group, 1989; U.S. General Accounting Office, 1990), researchers universalized the results beyond what the data warranted. Because the studies were done on males only and because the differing levels of hormones in males and females frequently cause significantly different interactions with drugs in the two sexes, this extrapolation from the study population of males only to the entire human species is inaccurate and inappropriate. A liberal feminist would argue that adding women to the original research design would correct this bias.

Applications of liberal feminism to current research agendas and their translation into practice and products might lead to the following sorts of changes: Equal numbers of women would be involved in setting the research agenda for the Human Genome Initiative or Project, which constitutes an attempt to sequence (find the chemical structure in terms of base pairs of DNA) of all 23 pairs of human chromosomes. The premise undergirding the project is that defects in genes cause diseases and syndromes. Knowing the exact location of each gene on the chromosome and its molecular structure (which can be discovered through gene sequencing) is the basis for transgenic species, correction of genes, and other biotechnologies.

Women scientists would have equal access to the grant moneys and sequencing equipment provided by the HGI, instead of the current male dominance of such resources. Because of their awareness of potential androcentric bias such as the possibility of increased interest in mapping genes for diseases causing increased mortality and morbidity in men, both men and women scientists would strive to eliminate such bias from research designs and interpretations of data. In attempts to assess the benefits of new or improved species developed through biotechnology, impacts on women's lives would be considered. For example, liberal feminists would ask whether the new, larger vegetables really have the nutritive value and taste of the biologically unmodified species, and that this be considered along with factors such as resistance to pests and higher yield per acre.

Liberal feminism suggests that equal numbers of men and women would develop new reproductive technologies. Liberal feminists view the cesarean as a life-saving technique developed to aid women who have difficulty in childbearing, and emergency obstetric care as an inalienable right of all women in the world, which often is kept from them because the health needs of men and children are considered before those of women. Liberal feminists note that in many countries, women often die in childbirth because they can not get emergency obstetrical care without the approval of their male relatives.

In contrast to the current situation in which most fertility technologies such as hormone injections, superovulation, in vitro fertilization, and gamete intrafallopian transfer (GIFT) center on the female, while the sperm count/assessment is the primary technology for the male, under liberal feminism the number and degree of invasiveness of the technologies would be the same for both men and women. Similarly, equal numbers of kinds of contraceptives with similar risks would be developed for both men and women.

In these examples, I have not "accidentally omitted" discussions of power, class, race, and other differences between men and women, among women, among men, or between nations. Suggesting that having more contraceptives that work on men's bodies without a discussion of the fact that it is women, not men, who become pregnant, the power dynamics involved when men control contraceptive use in a male-dominated society, the average income differential between most men and most women, and other relevant factors is consonant with liberal feminism and the scientific method. This liberal feminist presentation appears value-neutral, positivistic, and objective.

In contrast to liberal feminism, all other feminist theories call into question the fundamental assumptions underlying the scientific method, its corollaries of objectivity and value neutrality, or its implications. They reject individualism for a social construction of knowledge and question positivism and the possibility of objectivity obtained by value neutrality. Many also imply that men and women may conduct scientific research differently, although each theory posits a different cause for the gender distinction.

SOCIALIST FEMINISM

Socialist feminism, in contrast to liberal feminism, rejects individualism and positivism as approaches to knowledge. Marxist critiques, which form the historical precursors and foundations for socialist-feminist critiques, view all knowledge, including science, as socially constructed and emerging from practical human involvement in production. Since knowledge is a productive activity of human beings, it cannot be objective and value-free because the basic categories of knowledge are shaped by human purposes and values. During the twentieth century in the United States, according to Marxism, scientific knowledge was determined by capitalism, the prevailing mode of production, and reflected the interests of the dominant class.

Feminist critics (Bleier, 1984, 1986; Fee, 1982; Haraway, 1978; Hein, 1981; Hubbard, 1979) have discussed the extent to which the emphasis on sex-differences research in the neurosciences and endocrinology (when in fact for most traits there are no differences or only very small mean differences characterized by a large range of overlap between the sexes), and on the search for genetic bases to justify sex-role specialization and the division of labor, originates from the desire to find a biological basis for the social inequality between the sexes. The measurement of hormone levels in homosexuals compared with heterosexuals, the search for anatomical differences between the brains of homosexuals and heterosexuals, and the search for a "gene" for homosexuality are attempts to separate biological from environmental determinants and to seek biological bases for the discriminatory treatment against homosexuals (Birke, 1986). One can imagine that a society free from inequality between the sexes and lacking homophobia would not view research on sex differences and sexual orientation differences as valid scientific endeavors. The fact that our society supports such research indicates the extent to which the values of society and of scientists influence scientific inequity and "objectivity."

By emphasizing the social construction of knowledge, Marxism implies that dichotomies such as nature/culture, subjective/objective, and diffuse/focused, methods that distance the observer from the object of study, and the privileging of double-blind studies may not be the only, or even the best, ways to obtain scientific knowledge. It emphasizes interdisciplinary methods, active participation of subjects in research, and qualitative methods as superior ways to study health problems.

The billions of dollars spent on the Human Genome Initiative would be interpreted by Marxists as reflecting the interests of the dominant class. The focus on genes and the considerable publicity that surrounds the isolation and copying of "disease genes" suggest to most laypeople not only that most disease is biologically determined but more specifically that it is genetically caused. This diverts valuable research dollars away from environmental causes of, and contributions to, disease, and away from public health, long demonstrated to be more effective in eradicating most communicable, and other, diseases than the high tech solutions developed by medical research. Centering on genes also places responsibility on the individual and takes it away from the system and broader society.

The decisions regarding which products are developed from the numerous patented genes isolated and sequenced by the biotechnology industries fall more under the influence of capitalist interests in profit margins than the needs of people in developing countries for nutritious foods or the health and medical interests of the public as a whole. For example, Monsanto owns a patent covering all genetically engineered cotton seeds and plants, and genes governing Alzheimer's disease have been patented by Duke University (King & Stabinsky, 1999).

In most universities and biotechnology corporations, most genes sequenced and isolated are patented so that the university, corporation, and/or in rare cases the scientist reserves the right to the financial profits that may be derived from this intellectual property. If patents are granted, other researchers are prohibited from using the genes or gene sequences without obtaining a license from the patent holder. The patent holder researcher is free to charge a fee of any amount or to deny use to anyone for up to 20 years (often longer if the invention is modified and additional patents are sought), thus limiting research completely or to wealthy corporate or institutional researchers. For example, in order to gain a monopoly on the development of new antibacterial agents, Human Genome Sciences has patented the entire genomes of certain bacteria that can cause serious diseases in humans (King & Stabinsky, 1999).

If granted for genes or gene sequences, patents may promote secrecy in research since once something is public, it is no longer patentable. Such secrecy may restrict collaborative research. Equally important, it will restrict the peer review of the research evaluation by competent professionals in two ways. First, researchers will wait to publish results until they have patents. For example, the Roslin Institute in Scotland did not announce the cloning of Dolly until it had applied for patents on cloned sheep. The University of California at Berkeley signed a 5-year, $25 million research deal with Novartis, the Swiss biotechnology company, in which the company has 30 days to revise articles and delay publication for an additional 90 days to give it time to determine whether it wants Berkeley to file patents on any of the findings. The National Institutes of Health recommended that universities avoid publication delays of more than 2 months (Blumenstyk, 1998). Second, other researchers cannot attempt to replicate experimental results unless they can afford to pay the patent fee.

Such intellectual property rights function as a form of privatization (Mohanty, 1997). They permit decisions about which genes will be "developed" (used for research, ultimately to be spliced into foods, or manufactured in multiple copies to replace "defective" genes) to be made in the private sector rather than in the public realm. This results in capitalist interests in the bottom line, rather than public needs and interests, dictating which "products" are developed. Tax dollars support much of this basic research, including the basic research of the HGI, responsible for sequencing and isolating disease genes in humans. Taxes also underwrite the Department of Agriculture, where much basic research on genetic engineering in crops and plants began, and the Food and Drug Administration (FDA), which tests safety and efficacy of new drugs and products developed and synthesized by pharmaceutical companies from plant extract. In the patenting of intellectual property, rights (and profits) get transferred from the public, which paid for the research, to the private company, institution, or individual who controls the patent. Socialist feminists might view this as a transfer from the pockets of the working class, who pay the taxes to underwrite federal research, to the patent holders in the private sector who will reap massive profits, serving the interests of bourgeois capitalists.

Socialist-feminist critiques become most visible in their application to specific biotechnologies and reproductive technologies. The current state of medical knowledge, as critiqued by socialist feminists, would view the distribution of medical services as developed to perpetuate the capitalist system by maintaining inequalities in the distribution of wealth, services, and rights. Poor women and their babies in the United States have higher mortality rates than women with resources. Many studies have shown that wealthy women receive more cesareans than poor women, and receive better health services in general. Quality medical care itself is premised on the ability to pay. Additionally, the capitalist system makes childbirth into a commodity. The high percentage of hospital services in obstetrical care means that surgical procedures provide more profit than natural birth, which requires higher expenditures of time in a system where time equals money. Emergency obstetrical care should be extended to all women in society, regardless of their ability to pay, while women of resources should be protected from the exploitation of a profit-oriented medical system.

Socialist feminism explains the economic exchanges and inequities that occur surrounding reproductive technologies in the United States and the world. The capabilities opened by in vitro fertilization have led to an industry in which poor women are paid to gestate the developing fetus, who may represent the genetic offspring of a rich man and a woman who does not wish to and/or cannot carry a pregnancy to term—the so-called Baby M phenomenon (Raymond, 1991). A California judge ruled that the woman gestating the fetus derived from another woman's egg is comparable to a baby sitter and that the egg donor is the biological mother (Hubbard, 1995). On a worldwide scale, particularly in India and China, amniocentesis is used for sex selection to abort more female than male children, because traditionally in those cultures sons are valued more, partially because of their economic contribution to the family income and to the care of their elderly parents. A person born in an overdeveloped country consumes about 30 times as much as a person in an underdeveloped country (Corea, 1991). Despite the fact that children born in industrialized, first-world countries use more of the world's resources, women from first-world countries, especially middle-class ones, are encouraged to have children, while women in third-world countries are sterilized against their will. Infertility becomes the issue in first-world countries (Klein, 1989; Muller, 1992), while fertility signals the problem in developing countries (Eschen & Whittaker, 1993).

Socialist feminism describes how women, oppressed by both class and gender, have an advantageous and more comprehensive view of reality. Because of their oppression, they have an interest in perceiving problems with the status quo and the science and knowledge produced by the dominant class and gender. Simultaneously, their position requires them to understand the science and condition of the dominant group in order to survive. Thus, the standpoint of the oppressed comprehends and includes that of the dominant group, so it is more accurate.

An example that might be cast as socialist feminism is the work of grassroots women's groups dedicated to bringing national attention to breast cancer and its potential causes and treatments currently overlooked by the medical and basic research establishments. In 1992, the Women's Community Cancer Project presented *A Woman's Cancer Agenda: The Demands* to the National Cancer Institute and the U.S. government and asked for alternative treatments and research into environmental causes for the breast cancer epidemic, in addition to the radiation, chemotherapy, and high tech medical focus of current treatments and research. Dissatisfied with the research direction and solutions provided by the modern medical establishment, the National Breast Cancer Coalition, made up of more than 250 organizations nationwide, presented the President and First Lady on October 18, 1993, with petitions containing 2.6 million signatures demanding a comprehensive strategy plan to end the breast cancer epidemic (WCCP, 1994).

Their demands raise the question of whose interests are advanced when cancer research focuses on genes, cells, and hormones. For example, Myriad Genetics owns patents on human genes that, when damaged, lead to breast cancer (King & Stabinsky, 1999). Considerable media attention surrounded the isolation and copying in 1994 of the BRCA1 gene, located on chromosome 17q12-21, which causes an 85% risk of breast cancer when it mutates (Shattuck-Edens et al., 1995), and the subsequent isolation and sequencing of the BRCA2 gene. This focus came at the expense of attention to behavioral, social, and environmental causes, and suggested that most breast cancer is genetically caused. This focus also shifts responsibility from society as a whole to individuals.

The reality is that only 5–10% of breast cancer is inherited and that the BRCA1 and 2 genes are responsible for only half of the inherited cases (King, Rowell, & Love, 1993). This leaves 90 or 95% of breast cancer cases unaccounted for by the BRCA1 and 2 genes and points to the role caused by social, behavioral, and environmental factors. The incidence of breast cancer has increased 1% per year since 1940 (Harris, Lippman, Veronesi, & Willett, 1992). This fact, coupled with studies from the 1970s that documented a fivefold variation in breast cancer rates around the world (Armstrong & Doll, 1975) and that the incidence of breast cancer in Japanese women who migrate from their low-incidence home country to the United States becomes that of U.S. women, suggests that factors besides genetics are significant for the disease. Inclusion of social, psychological, and public health perspectives is needed for a more comprehensive research base to explore also why poor women and women of color in the United States have higher death rates from breast cancer than White, middle- and upper-class women.

Yet very little research centers on environmental causes of breast cancer. Socialist-feminist analyses would suggest that this dearth of research into environmental causes of breast cancer serves capitalist interests. Industry might have to stop its environmental pollution or clean up areas it previously polluted, if research definitively linked some industrial wastes to breast cancer.

AFRICAN AMERICAN/WOMANIST AND RACIAL/ETHNIC FEMINISM

Like socialist feminism, African American/womanist or racial/ethnic feminism, based on African American critiques of a Eurocentric approach to knowledge, also rejects individualism and positivism for social construction as an approach to knowledge. African American critiques also question methods that distance the observer from the object of study, thereby denying a facet of the social construction of knowledge.

African American critiques maintain that race is the primary oppression and view the scientific enterprise as a function of White Eurocentric interests. As Harding underlines in *Is Science Multicultural?* (1998), much of the scientific development of Europe occurred at the expense of colonization and de-development of European colonies. These colonies in Southern continents served as scientific laboratories and as sources of raw materials and cheap labor. Racism, colonialism, and capitalism underpinned European scientific achievements. In the United States, early colonists decimated native populations with infectious diseases, actively destroying their cultures, while appropriating agricultural, mining, and engineering skills that permitted the colonists to survive in the new world.

During the twentieth century, race was a factor in genetic testing in the United States. Some of the earliest applications of gene testing centered around sickle cell disease testing in the 1960s and 1970s, concentrated primarily in the African American population in the United States. The use of test results proved to have negative consequences in terms of denial of insurance benefits, employment opportunities, and stigmas due to misunderstanding of the differences between carriers of the gene and individuals with the disease. This large-scale project recalls former scientific/medical initiatives such as the Tuskegee Syphilis Experiment from 1932 to 1972 in the United States (Jones, 1981) or the testing of high-estrogen birth control pills in Puerto Rico in the late 1960s (Zimmerman et al., 1980), in which the bodies of people of color became the test sites for drugs and diseases thought to be too dangerous for testing in the White population. Because of these events, ethnic populations have been in the forefront voicing the potential problems surrounding privacy issues and who has access to the information derived from genetic testing.

In contemporary health care research, for example, the identification of AIDS by group characteristics such as sexual orientation, class, and race—gay males, IV drug users, and Haitian immigrants—rather than risk behaviors, demonstrates the ability of the dominant heterosexual, White middle class to label the disease as "other" and distort the research agenda. The intensive study of crack cocaine and other substance abuse in women (primarily poor and African American) seeking prenatal care in public health settings, coupled with the lack of study of such abuse in women obtaining prenatal care in private-practice settings, demonstrates similar dominance and distortion (Chasnoff, Landress, & Barrett, 1990).

Not surprisingly, some view the Human Genome Initiative as providing a further opportunity for genocide of ethnic populations. The Human Genome Diversity Project, which samples indigenous and other "vanishing" tribal populations, may be viewed from an ethnic perspective as an attempt to preserve genes, while allowing the peoples themselves to become extinct. Some have questioned the motives of Axys Pharmaceuticals, with its application for patents on cells and genes of New Guinea tribes, to use in developing treatments against viruses to which the tribes may have developed immunities (King & Stabinsky, 1999).

RiceTec has obtained a patent on basmati rice, grown in India for thousands of years, so that farmers anywhere in the world (including India) must now purchase a license from the company to grow the rice

(King & Stabinsky, 1999). Similarly, genetic samples of indigenous varieties of plants and animals from developing Southern countries are preserved by scientists from the Northern continents, while they simultaneously introduce Northern agricultural methods, including genetically engineered crops, that destroy acres of habitat and species at the rate of one per day from the tropical forests in many developing countries (Shiva, 1989). Economic profits anticipated from extracts from plants with herbal healing powers justify the use of high technology methods such as remote sensing to map out medicinal plant habitats (Mooney, 1998).

Racism and sexism become intertwining oppressions that provide African American women with a different perspective and standpoint from that of either White women or African American men (Collins, 1990). In the absence of universal health coverage in the United States, differential survival statistics for women from diverse socioeconomic backgrounds and races stand as the norm. The "poor, in general, have a 10 to 15 percent lower cancer survival rate regardless of race. . . . The five year survival rate after breast cancer is 75 percent in white women compared to 63 percent for African American women" (Altman, 1996, pp. 37–38). Black women, and their babies, in the United States have higher mortality rates than their White counterparts. Race is a major factor in determining the quality of medical care a woman receives in the United States. Caesareans are performed most often on White, middle-class women who also receive better prenatal care than Black women. It is primarily White, middle-class women who have objected to the abuse of caesarean section. Such critique has not necessarily reflected the views of many Black women giving birth in hospitals who prefer medical intervention over neglect and lack of access to health care. The tremendous heritage of African American midwifery has been systematically exploited, as has that of midwifery as a whole in the United States. African American midwives were coopted into the health care system in southern states such as South Carolina (Altekruse & Rosser, 1992), where their knowledge was supervised and controlled. Then they were systematically excluded from the medical system in the 1960s and replaced by inadequate services. Women of color giving birth are doubly oppressed, primarily by race, and secondarily by gender. Judgment on the value of cesareans cannot be made without a careful analysis of this context.

Socialist-feminist and African American feminist theories imply that women scientists, through a collective process of political and scientific struggle (Jaggar, 1983), might produce a science and knowledge different from that produced by men of any race or class. This research would provide a more accurate picture of reality since it would be based in the experience of women, who hold a more comprehensive view because of their race, class, and gender. The National Black Women's Health Project, founded by Byllye Avery, exemplifies this view in its attempts to define health care issues and education from the standpoint of African American women.

ESSENTIALIST FEMINISM

Essentialist-feminist theory posits that women are different from men because of their biology, specifically their secondary sex characteristics and their reproductive systems. Frequently, essentialist feminism may extend to include gender differences in visual-spatial and verbal ability, aggression and other behavior, and other physical and mental traits based on prenatal or pubertal hormone exposure.

Essentialism and the sociobiology research supporting it were critiqued by feminist scientists (Bleier, 1979; Fausto-Sterling, 1992; Hubbard, 1979; Rosser, 1982) as providing biological evidence for differences in mental and behavioral characteristics between males and females. Essentialism was seen as a tool for conservatives who wished to keep women in the home and out of the workplace. More recently, feminists have reexamined essentialism from perspectives ranging from conservative to radical (Corea, 1985; Dworkin, 1983; MacKinnon, 1982, 1987; O'Brien, 1981; Rich, 1976), with a recognition that biologically based differences between the sexes might imply superiority and power for women in some arenas.

Essentialist feminism would imply that their biology—differential hormonal effects on the brain; the physical experiences of menstrual cycles, pregnancy, childbirth, lactation, and menopause; and/or other differing anatomical or physiological characteristics—would lead female scientists to use different methods to approach problems in science from those used by men.

Some of the differences described by scholars (Arnup, Levesque, & Pierson, 1990; Ehrenreich & English, 1978; Sullivan & Weitz, 1988; Wertz & Wertz, 1977) between the way that female midwives and male physicians solve difficulties arising during labor and childbirth might be perceived as essentialist. For example, the emphasis of midwives on emotional and spiritual support for the laboring mother, while taking time to massage the perineum during the emergence of the baby's head, might be construed as arising from the remembrance by the midwife of how her own body felt during labor and childbirth. In contrast, the male physician, never having personally undergone labor or childbirth, favors drugs to deaden the pain and surgical procedures such as episiotomies to speed the delivery, thereby shortening the ordeal.

Essentialist-feminist critiques suggest that knowledge about birth must be developed with a respect for women's knowledge of their bodies and their innate ability to give birth. The current system, with a high rate of cesarean sections, is based on a patriarchal medical system, which assumes that the female body is a flawed and inferior version of the male body. This system has contributed to women's alienation from their bodies and the notion that they cannot give birth normally, resulting in high cesarean rates. What is not recognized is that the differences between males and females result in women's superior abilities in assisting childbirth. A system of childbirth care developed out of women's ways of knowing would include considerations for relationships beginning at birth: between a woman and her baby, her partner, her birth attendant, and any other people she invites to share the bonding of birth. Dualist constructs such as mind/body must be amended by women's more holistic ways of thinking and being. When these rifts are healed, women can give birth safely in the presence of people they love, and the need for surgical intervention drops (Good Maust, 1994).

Some individuals who might be categorized as essentialist, and possibly as conservative, push for more research that would result in discoveries such as the BRCA1 and 2 genes. This focus on genetic causes of cancer, which may result, in the case of the BRCA1 and 2 genes, in the testing of some families and in women who have the genes having radical mastectomies before any sign of cancer is detected, might be supported by conservative essentialist feminists. Essentialists, who might be seen as extreme biological determinists, would push for more women scientists to be involved in this research to ensure that more HGI dollars would be directed toward isolation of genetic diseases that are particularly problematic for women. For similar reasons, they would want women involved in the development of reproductive technologies.

Some of the more radical essentialists identify with ecofeminism. Merchant (1979) and Griffin (1978) begin their documentation of science's historical roots with the seventeenth-century shift from an organic hermetic approach to science, in which men revered and saw themselves as part of the environment and nature (and saw women as identified with nature), to a mechanistic, objective approach in which the objective distance endorsed men's domination and exploitation of the environment (and women) (Keller, 1985). Ecofeminists have made explicit the connection between the domination of both women and the environment through the androcentrism of modern science (Harding, 1986; King, 1983, 1989). Such ecofeminists would propose that women, because of their essential identification with nature, would develop biotechnologies less harmful to the environment.

EXISTENTIALIST FEMINISM

It is the value that society assigns to biological differences between males and females that has led women to play the role of the Other (Tong, 1989); it is not the biological differences themselves. The philosophical origins of existentialist feminism emphasize that it is man's conception of woman as "other" that has led to his willingness to dominate and exploit her. It results in the view of the male norm in drug testing and the view of the female as "other" or deviant from the male norm. Some examples suggest that man's view of woman as other stretches to the point that his interactions with and treatment of her are similar to his interactions with another, lower species.

The methodological implications arising out of existentialist feminism are that a society that emphasizes gender differences would produce a science that emphasizes sex differences. In such a society, men and women might be expected to create very different sciences because of the social construction of both gender and science. The possibility of a gender-free or gender-neutral (positivist) science evolving in such a society is virtually nil. Elizabeth Fee (1982) summed up the situation very well: She states that a sexist society should be expected to develop a sexist science. Conceptualizing a feminist science from within our society is "like asking a medieval peasant to imagine the theory of genetics or the production of a space capsule" (p. 31).

Existentialist feminism provides a theoretical explanation for the current significant gender differential in research and treatment in cardiovascular disease in men compared with women. Because this society defines women as "other" in contrast to men, the fact that heart disease strikes men at an earlier age than women, served as sufficient reason to direct the vast majority of research funds and treatment protocols toward men. The similar frequency of heart disease in women compared with men was ignored since difference in age rather than similarity of frequency was emphasized in keeping with the definition of women as "other." This emphasis on difference resulted in extreme bias in research, such as women's exclusion from 82% of studies between 1960 and 1991 of clinical trials for medications to prevent myocardial infarctions (Gurwitz, Nananda, & Avorn, 1992), and an in-hospital death rate for women 10 times that of men after angioplasty (Kelsey et al., 1993).

Existential-feminist critiques imply that differences between men and women are socially constructed by a patriarchal society and engraved at the moment of birth. The cesarean operation is an outcome of a technologically oriented society that has developed around a male obsession with tools and the need to dominate and subdue nature. The moment of birth is a rite of passage in which a society inscribes its primary attributes; the components of hospital birth are a part of a medical system that defines women out of the moment of birth and asserts male dominance over the supremely natural process of childbirth. This defining out of women results in "nature" (woman) defined as inadequate and in need of remedy with the tools available to the medical system—cesarean sections, episiotomies, and forceps. This ensures that all present at birth partake in the construction of a patriarchal, technological society.

Ecofeminists coming from an existentialist perspective would suggest that they should be involved in biotechnology and reproductive technology development, not because of their biological essentialism, but because they and other species have been dominated and treated as "other" by men and male scientists. Individuals, both male and female, from the disability rights movements have made arguments similar to those of essentialist feminists for why they should be actively involved in the HGI and other biotechnology developments (Saxton, 1996). They also point out that the potential and actual elimination of disabilities caused by genetic defects increases pressure for persons with disabilities to be perceived as "other" and decreases pressure for the society to provide services for disabled people.

The negative impacts of the HGI appear likely to fall disproportionately upon women. It is women who will undergo much of the prenatal genetic testing and screening, perhaps on a less-than-voluntary basis. Women's bodies will again become the site over which battles may be fought regarding whether and when abortions should be given, if a fetus has a genetic condition that may result in a disability. Women will be the ones likely to serve as primary caretakers for congenitally disabled children in a society with shrinking resources. Also, the bulk of genetic counselors are women. They must grapple with delivering difficult, technical information to patients; they also will face changing relationships with physicians and other health care professionals as genetics increasingly plays a dominant role in health care. Because of their biological capability to give birth, women have been assigned the existentialist role of other and caretaker.

PSYCHOANALYTIC FEMINISM

Based on the Freudian prejudice that anatomy is destiny, psychoanalytic theory assumes that biological sex will lead to different ways for boys and girls to resolve the Oedipus and castration complexes that arise during the phallic stage of normal sexual development. Rejecting the biological determinism in Freud, Dinnerstein (1977) and Chodorow (1978) in particular have used an aspect of psychoanalytic theory known as object-relations theory to examine the construction of gender and sexuality during the Oedipal stage of psychosexual development, which usually results in male dominance. They conclude that the gender differences resulting in male dominance can be traced to the fact that in our society, women are the primary caretakers for most infants and children.

Keller (1982, 1985) in particular applied the work of Chodorow and Dinnerstein to suggest how science has become a masculine province, populated mostly by men, and in its choice of experimental topics, use of male subjects for experimentation, interpretation, and theorizing from data, as well as the practice and applications of science undertaken by scientists. Keller (1982, 1985) suggests that since the scientific method stresses objectivity, rationality, distance, and autonomy of the observer from the object of study (i.e., the positivist neutral observer), individuals who feel comfortable with independence, autonomy, and distance will be most likely to become scientists. Feminists have suggested that the objectivity and rationality of science are synonymous with a male approach to the physical, natural world.

According to psychoanalytic feminism, women researchers as exemplified by June Goodfield or by Nobel laureate Barbara McClintock might be more likely to use approaches that shorten the distance between them as observers and their objects of study, might develop a relationship with their objects of study, and might appear to be less objective. Comparisons of approaches to clinical research undertaken by nurses and physicians reveal that nurses favor qualitative, patient-involved approaches, while physicians favor quantitative, double-blind studies. Complex social, economic, and gender interactions have resulted in the female-dominated profession of nursing emphasizing caring, qualitative, patient-centered, and involved research (Mulligan, 1992; Noddings, 1984), and the male-dominated medical profession using "objective" quantitative research where distance is maintained between the patient and the physician researcher (Altekruse & Rosser, 1992; Morantz-Sanchez, 1988). Although psychoanalytic feminism may oversimplify these historical, economic, class, and gender complexities, it is compatible with the differential research approaches of nursing and medicine.

Psychoanalytic feminism implies that less separation between the developers and users of bio- and reproductive technologies would benefit both scientists and the women and other people who experience the effects of the technologies. For example, psychoanalytic feminists suggest that the medical science developed out of the patriarchal systems of thought that emphasize distance, autonomy, separation, and independence leads to a high rate of cesarean sections. This has its roots in gender socialization. If men were caretakers of children, this kind of separation would not occur. Men need to be more involved in childbirth, in the early bonding that happens in the hours after birth, and a part of the sexual experience of childbirth, since it has been shown that nipple stimulation and intercourse facilitate birth. Reliance on caesareans reflects the distance of science from the recognition that birth is a heterosexual experience involving two partners. If fathers were brought back into childbirth, were allowed to experience childbirth, and became a part of bonding, they would be better caretakers of their children and would rear children who tended to value relationship and intimacy, helping to bring about a science of birth that eventually would contribute to a less alienated society.

The current medical/research model has led to the need for a group of professionals, the genetic counselors who explain the results and implications of tests and technologies to "consumers" who then must decide whether to have a mastectomy because they carry the mutant copies of the BCRA1 and 2 genes, abort a child when amniocentesis suggests that it would have spina bifida, or elect not to have "genetic" children at all because of the results of tests indicating a certain statistical probability that genes they carry may lead to the production of a "defective" offspring. Psychoanalytic feminists would propose less separation between researchers and users by having women, people with disabilities, and individuals from developing countries involved in the design- and funding-decision stages of genetic research. This involvement would lead to more appropriate technologies, while also informing "consumers" more accurately of the implications of the technologies.

Even the International Monetary Fund (IMF) and World Bank have recognized that one reason for the failure of many "development" projects, including genetically engineered crops, was the failure to include the population of women who traditionally worked with the crops in the planning and implementation of the project. While continuing to impose other Northern, agricultural ideas, including the use of genetically engineered crops, development officials have learned that Eurocentric ideas regarding gender divisions of labor and land tenure in agriculture may lead to failed projects when imposed on Southern continents. They now attempt to include women in planning and implementing agricultural development projects. Involving women in such projects and men in childbirth and childrearing resonates with psychoanalytic feminist theories.

RADICAL FEMINISM

Radical feminism maintains that women's oppression is the first, most widespread, and deepest oppression (Jaggar & Rothenberg, 1992). Scientific institutions, practice, and knowledge are particularly male-dominated and have been documented by many feminists (Bleier, 1984; Fee, 1983; Griffin, 1978; Haraway, 1978, 1989; Hubbard, 1990; Keller, 1985; Merchant, 1979; Rosser, 1990) to be especially effective patriarchal tools to control and harm women. Radical feminism rejects most scientific theories, data, and experiments precisely because they not only exclude women but also are not women-centered.

Radical feminism deviates considerably from other feminisms in its view of how beliefs are legitimated as knowledge. A successful strategy that women use to obtain reliable knowledge and correct distortions of patriarchal ideology is the consciousness-raising group (Jaggar, 1983). Using their personal experiences as a basis, women meet together in communal, nonhierarchical groups to examine their experiences in order to determine what counts as knowledge (MacKinnon, 1987). The Boston Women's Health Book Collective and other women's health collectives serve as examples of women's attempts to understand their health experiences through a collective coming together. *Our Bodies, Ourselves* (1978, 1984, 1992, 1998) represents a product of their collective knowledge based on those experiences.

Because of the belief of radical feminists in connection and a conception of the world as an organic whole, they reject dualistic, hierarchical approaches, and dichotomies that fragment the organic whole of reality. Cyclicity as a conception of time and thinking as an upward spiral seem more appropriate ways to study a world in which everything is connected in a process of constant change (Daly, 1978, 1984). Under radical feminism, the female body, with its cyclicity of menstruation, serves as the ideal model for other, nonreproductive hormones and continual biological change (Hoffman, 1982); the static male body is a deviation from the female norm.

Many radical feminists believe that because of their connection to the living and nonliving world, women can know things by relying on intuition and/or spiritual powers. Women's knowledge through experience of what is health would be viewed as superior to that of male physicians based on medical studies. Radical feminists vary in their belief as to whether the special ways of knowing of women are due to their biology (Daly, 1978; Griffin, 1978), their common social experiences as an oppressed group (Belenky, Clinchy, Goldberger, & Tarule, 1986), or both.

If radical feminists found biotechnologies and reproductive technologies acceptable, the requests for their development, research design, and applications would originate from consciousness-raising groups in which women discussed their experiences to determine which, if any, technologies should be developed. Radical-feminist critiques might suggest that childbirth would be safer if no men were involved at all. The cesarean operation is a part of a patriarchal system of medical care and a result of the active elimination of knowledge of midwifery and women's knowledge of healing in the witch burnings of the fifteenth century (Ehrenreich & English, 1978). It also was designed in the first place to extract a living baby from a dead woman's body, and it continues to be used in the best interests of the baby. Rates of mortality and morbidity for women are consistently higher for cesarean birth than for vaginal birth. Childbirth in institutions is a part of the active oppression of women, where their knowledge, dignity, and power are violently abused in high rates of cesareans, episiotomies, and use of forceps. Women are robbed of the exhilaration and empowerment possible in childbirth by patriarchally oriented doctors who do caeserens (Good Maust, 1996). When women's own knowledge of the body and their experiences of childbirth are used to develop expertise in childbirth, the rates of cesareans should decrease.

Although the origin and development of the technology of the contraceptive device known as the cervical cap certainly cannot be traced to women's consciousness-raising groups, its recent testing in the United States might be seen as an example of the impact and use of such groups. Reintroduced into the United States from Europe in the 1970s, the cervical cap was required to go through the Food and Drug Administration (FDA) approval process (Muller, 1992), since it had been off the market in the United States for several decades and women's health activists had requested its reintroduction. In addition to the typical route for approval of clinical trials and double-blind studies, the FDA permitted women's health clinics and collectives to serve as test sites for approval of the device. Since such clinics and collectives often originated from women's consciousness-raising groups, this might be construed as a glimpse of how radical feminists might affect bio- and reproductive technologies.

LESBIAN SEPARATISM AND QUEER THEORY

Lesbian separatism, often seen as an offshoot of radical feminism, would suggest that separation from men is necessary in a patriarchal society for females to understand their experiences and explore the potentials of science and the impacts of reproductive technologies. Without obstetrics and its emphasis on procreation and heterosexual activity, research, diagnosis, and treatment in women's health might look quite different. The theory of separatism suggests the possible evolution of women-centered research agendas, created and carried out by female researchers, using women as participant-subjects, to develop health promotion and disease prevention for women, in the absence of patriarchal hierarchies and strictures.

Lesbian-separatist theory provides a context that reveals why a patriarchal society encourages the use of technologies for sex selection that lead to the abortion of female fetuses, why a heterosexist society permits only heterosexual women who are married to men to receive artificial insemination, and why significant research dollars are poured into the search for "gay genes." In addition to explaining these current practices, lesbian-separatist feminism suggests that in the absence of a patriarchal society that enforces compulsory heterosexuality (Rich, 1976), very different bio- and reproductive technologies might be developed, if they would be permitted at all.

Separatist critiques of childbirth might emphasize its need to be separated from its moorings in heterosexual reproduction. This implies a rejection of both fertility technologies and childbirth that takes place in patriarchal institutions. Artificial insemination and childbirth can be women-centered processes. For example, resources might be put into research on parthenogenesis, so that two women might have a child whose genetic parentage they would share.

Queer and transgender theories question links between sex, gender, and sexual orientation (Butler, 1990). They raise additional challenges about the links between gender and economic, racial, and dominance factors in our society. As Judith Butler (1990, 1992, 1994) argues, the very act of defining a gender identity excludes or devalues some bodies and practices, while simultaneously obscuring the constructed character of gender identity; describing gender identity creates a norm. New reproductive technologies cause us to redefine mothering into fine distinctions: genetic mother, gestational mother, and social/rearing mother. In the near future, technologies may permit men to give birth, thus permitting the man in a heterosexual couple to serve as the gestating parent. Technologies eventually may allow two men or two women to have children that are genetically theirs. In these senses, the technologies could break gender stereotypes and norms of gender identities, opening the door to freedom. In contrast, the existence of such technologies may reinforce an emphasis on sex and "nature" over gender and "nurture," leading to reification of traditional gender roles.

POSTMODERN FEMINISM

Liberal feminism suggests that women have a unified voice and can be universally addressed (Gunew, 1990). According to postmodernism, "the values of reason, progress, and human rights endorsed by the Enlightenment have shown their dark side" (Tanesini, 1999, p. 239). In postmodernism, the self is no longer regarded as "masterful, universal, integrated, autonomous, and self-constructed; rather it is socially constructed by ideology, discourse, the structure of the unconscious, and/or language" (Rothfield, 1990, p. 132). Postmodernism dissolves the universal subject, and postmodern feminism dissolves the possibility that women speak in a unified voice or that they can be universally addressed. Although one woman may share certain characteristics and experiences with other women because of her biological sex, her particular race, class, and sexual differences compared with other women, along with the construction of gender that her country and society give to someone living in her historical period, prevent the universalizing of her experiences to women in general. At least some postmodern feminists (e.g., Cixous & Clement, 1986; Kristeva, 1984, 1987) suggest that women, having been marginalized by a dominant male discourse, may be in a privileged position, that of outsider to the discourse, to find the holes in what appears solid, sure, and unified. Otherwise, the dominant discourse threatens to rigidify all thought in society along previously established lines. Postmodern-feminist theories imply that no universal research agenda or application of bio- or reproductive technologies will be appropriate and that various women will have different reactions to the technologies, depending on their own class, race, sexual orientation, country, and other factors.

This theory may explain why rates of cesareans cannot be compared across extremely diverse populations. That rates are extremely high in Brazil and very low in Japan does not mean that all rates should be low. Women's bodies, as well as their cultural surroundings, may be differently constructed, both socially and biologically. Within each society many differences between women in race, class, and ethnicity can result in differential biologies as well. Medical knowledge about birth and cesareans cannot be generalized to all women, and any program or health policy must be designed with a knowledge of multilayered differences. This means that to one woman the experience of cesarean may be a matter of choice and empowerment, while to another it may mean death or incapacitation for a period of time.

Because postmodernism recognizes different, yet valid, standpoints from which various individuals view the same activities, the theory often is criticized (Butler, 1992) for leading to political inactivity. Postmodern feminists would be unlikely to have a unified position on a biological research agenda, applications of various reproductive technologies, or whether bio- or reproductive technologies should be pursued at all. Postmodern feminism may explain why many feminists oppose in vitro fertilization and other reproductive technologies, while many women eagerly seek them out in their desire to overcome infertility and produce "perfect" children.

POSTCOLONIAL FEMINISM

Beginning in 1947, following various campaigns of anticolonial resistance, often with an explicitly nationalist basis, many colonial empires formally dissolved, and previously colonized countries gained independence (Williams & Chrisman, 1994). Although the end of colonial rule created high hope for a proper postcolonial era, the extent to which the West had not relinquished control became clear quickly. The continuing Western influence, particularly in the economic arena, but also in the political, ideological, and military sectors, became known as neocolonialism by Marxists (Williams & Chrisman, 1994). Feminists have suggested that patriarchy dominates postcolonial and neocolonial, much as it dominated colonial, everyday life.

Not surprisingly, scientific research, biotechnologies, and reproductive technologies reflect the varying complex aspects of the interrelationship between developed and developing countries in general and between the particular cultures of colonized and colonizing countries. General themes include the underdevelopment of the Southern continents by Europe and the other Northern continents (Harding, 1993); ignoring, obscuring, or misappropriating earlier scientific achievements and history of countries in Southern continents; the fascination with so-called "indigenous science" (Harding, 1998); the idea that the culture, science, and technology of the colonizer or former colonizing country remain superior to those of the colony or postcolonial country; and the insistence that developing countries must restructure their local economies to become scientifically and technologically literate so they can join and compete in a global economy (Mohanty, 1997). In Northern, former colonizing countries, the concurrent restructuring effects of multinational corporations and other forces of globalization are evidenced in downsizing, privatization, and widening economic gaps between the poor and very wealthy. The particular forms and ways that these general themes take shape and play out vary, depending on the history, culture, geography, and length of colonization for both the colonized and colonizing countries.

Global medical knowledge (often referred to as cosmopolitan medicine to respect the various forms that medicine takes in a variety of nation-states) developed under conditions in which an available, impoverished labor force was important to sustain colonial systems of extraction of resources. The production of humans, not the health of women, was a major impetus to the particular shaping of medical knowledge. According to postcolonial-feminist critiques, under this system cesareans ensured the production of infants at the cost of the mortality or, more often, the morbidity of their mothers. The fact that women who undergo cesarean section have a 20–50% chance of developing an infection requires careful postpartum care involving follow-up medical supervision, the availability of antibiotics, and the presence of caregivers who can take over household tasks such as food preparation and childcare for older children (Good Maust, 1996).

In addition, global medical interests include the exportation of medical technology to areas that are poorly equipped to use or maintain the equipment. Increasing use of cesarean sections, which involve the use of imported technology, nonlocal pharmaceuticals, and nonlocal resources, is undertaken to the detriment of local systems of obstetrical care, which were developed over centuries. Obstetrical care is provided in inadequate, poorly designed clinics staffed by people who represent the interests of the state.

The conditions that lead to poor maternal health are perpetuated, leaving women to bear the human costs of reproduction of the labor force. The system of medical care is implemented to fix emergencies rather than contribute to health. The medical expertise in clinics was designed around the needs of first-world women (who can be found in all countries of the world). Women in this case are multiply oppressed: by their gender, by their social class, by their position vis-à-vis the state, and by a medical hegemony that perpetuates global economic interests.

The issues surrounding postcolonial science vary considerably between India and Kenya, for example. Although both India and Kenya were colonized by the British, the differences in indigenous cultures, geographies, and length of time since independence have led to remarkably different problems and uses of modern science and technology. In India, amniocentesis has been used for sex determination to abort undesired female fetuses. The particularities of Indian culture, economics, and religion, in which sons are highly valued, the elderly are cared for by sons, and dowry prices to find a good marriage partner for daughters can be very expensive, encourage this use of amniocentesis. In Kenya, in contrast, the indigenous culture, including polygamy, valuing of children in general, and agricultural production, discourages such sex selection and abortion.

As in many developing countries, in both Kenya and India genetically bred agricultural species have been introduced in the context of "green revolutions." Although increasing crop yields in the short run, these revolutions often prove ecologically and economically disastrous in the long run, particularly for women. For example, the introduction of hybrid corn and high-yielding varieties of wheat necessitates the introduction of Western farming methods such as use of tractors and harvesters. To plant the fields, forests must be cleared. As species are removed, biodiversity is lost. Also, these crops quickly deplete the soil of nutrients, which must be replaced by expensive fertilizers. The accompanying changes in the ecosystem lead to droughts and less water. Women must walk further each day to obtain water for their families; they must walk particularly far to obtain water unpolluted by agricultural runoff. Postcolonial feminism would suggest that indigenous peoples, including both individuals who have not left the country as well as the elite, educated individuals in the colonizing and other countries, should help to steer the research and applications of bio- and reproductive technologies.

CONCLUDING COMPARISONS AND CONTRASTS

Although all feminist theories encourage a questioning of current (patriarchal) assumptions about science and health research, the methods of study, and questions asked, each theory adds a layer of complexity to previously developed theories. In reaction to the growing knowledge that the diversity among women meant that the universalism suggested by liberal feminism was not appropriate to describe the experiences of all women, other feminist theories evolved. Although essentialist and existential feminism might be interpreted to imply that biological sex and its interpretation in our society provide an overriding similarity to the experiences of all women, other feminist theories suggest that other factors may be equally or more important than sex/gender. Among factors considered influential in interaction with gender are class (socialist feminism), race (African American feminism), and family dynamics (psychoanalytic). Postmodern and radical feminism question the very categories of knowledge, and postmodern feminism suggests that each woman in each society during a particular historical period may have a differing standpoint from which she views the world, as shaped by her race, class, and numerous other factors, including her gender. Postcolonial feminism, the focus of

Chapter 3, calls attention to the significance of the interrelationship between colonizing and colonized countries and the influence of a global
economy, restructuring, and patriarchy in each.

As biological research and its applications to bio- and reproductive
technologies have evolved, they too have become increasingly complex.
The lenses of feminist theories provide a variety of perspectives through
which such research and its implementation may be viewed to ensure
broader inclusion in both research design and application. These lenses
also provide glimpses of the power and political struggles surrounding
these technologies, which lead to potential dangers for women. Feminist
perspectives may signal early warnings for scientists and physicians who
may unwittingly participate in developments that harm people, especially
men of color and women.

Postcolonial Feminist Critiques: Windows on Biases in Western Science

POSTCOLONIAL FEMINIST THEORIES and critiques open windows to understanding new biases in science. The conscious de-development of Southern continents under colonization by countries in Northern continents (Harding, 1993, 1998; Shiva, 1991a) in the nineteenth and early twentieth centuries created a historical backdrop in which centuries of indigenous knowledge of the environment, health, and natural resources and appropriate technologies were erased. This and the conditions of colonization create an atmosphere that allows most Western/Northern scientists to fail to challenge the notions that Northern science, scientists, and technologies have everything to give and nothing to learn from science, scientists, and technologies of developing countries. Current practices such as the new laws and patents claimed through Trade Related Intellectual Property (TRIP) rights in the General Agreement on Tariffs and Trades (GATT) may exacerbate the conditions of this atmosphere. Splicing a gene into a seed variety cultivated for centuries by indigenous women makes the seed the property of the Northern scientist. The indigenous women must now purchase back the engineered seed at an exorbitant price if they wish to grow crops that can compete in a global economy (Shiva, 1997).

MODEL FOR CURRICULAR INTEGRATION OF POSTCOLONIAL PERSPECTIVES INTO SCIENCE

Considering ways to integrate the knowledge gained from postcolonial feminism into the science curriculum provides a means of ensuring that this critical information and perspective will reach the next generation of scientists. Previously I have developed models (Rosser, 1990, 1995) to

integrate theories of feminism and methods of women's studies into science and health courses in attempts to attract and retain more men of
color and women in science. I based the models for integration into the
sciences on experiences with curriculum transformation projects in ethnic
and women's studies over the past quarter century and on previous phase
models developed by scholars in other disciplines to chart the phases
through which changes occur in a variety of disciplines in diverse institutions (McIntosh, 1984; Schuster & Van Dyne, 1984; Tetreault, 1985).

The six-phase model I developed (Rosser, 1993, 1995) to explain the
process for integrating new scholarship on women into science courses
might serve as a useful starting point for the process of integrating information and insights from applying postcolonial feminist critiques. The
new model follows the format of the previous model (Rosser, 1995), with
new emphases on postcolonial perspectives:

> Phase I: Absence of indigenous science and scientists not noted
> Phase II: Recognition that since most scientists are Western/Northern
>   and male, the science they create may reflect a Eurocentric/
>   colonial as well as masculine perspective
> Phase III: Development of understanding through postcolonial cri-
>   tiques that Eurocentric/Northern, male biases and perspectives
>   may prevent recognition of contributions from other cultures
>   and standpoints
> Phase IV: Rediscovery of indigenous science and technology
> Phase V: Focus on the current science and technology of developing
>   countries
> Phase VI: Mutually beneficial interchanges and exchanges

In considering postcolonial perspectives and the process for inclusion of
science and technology from indigenous peoples and developing countries, the word "Western" or "Northern" is often used instead of or in
addition to "male" or "masculine," while "indigenous" or "developing"
is often used instead of or in addition to "women" or "feminist." This
suggests the often cited notion of the conflation of all inferiors by the
dominant group (Harding, 1986).

To the extent that science reflects the interests of the White, middle-
and upper-class Western/Northern male and that most scientists are also
personal representatives of that elite, many of the biases toward and
treatment of knowledge and individuals (whether women and/or formerly colonized) not from the dominant tradition will be similar. Scholars
from diverse backgrounds have noted this in examples ranging from the
overlap between Eurocentric and androcentric views, as described by

Africanists and feminists (Harding, 1986), through overlaps of capitalist and masculinist views (Rose, 1983, 1994), to orientalist and feminine coding for each of these others in different times and in different cultures (Said, 1978). I also have written about the risks of the M. Butterfly dilemma (Rosser, 1990) and recognize many of the limitations and risks of extrapolating a theory or model derived from the experiences of one group or identity to others. Postcolonial critiques centered on educational institutions also have dealt specifically with this issue (Altbach, 1971; Engber, 1996; Thiong'O, 1972; Viswanathan, 1987). Yet using the model I developed for integrating women into curricular content in the sciences may provide some useful insights for those wishing to integrate postcolonial perspectives into science.

After briefly explaining each phase, I include examples of key readings that led me to connect the critique with the particular phase. These might be used successfully in a faculty development workshop or in an upper-level science class to raise the issues pertinent to each phase.

Phase I: Absence of indigenous science and scientists not noted

Most of the science and medical curricula throughout North America and Europe remain in phase I. In this phase, faculty and students may not notice the absence of people from Africa, Latin America, and Asia from the theoretical and decision-making positions in the Euro-American scientific and medical establishment. Although aware of the quotas on immigration and movements of the U.S. Congress to stop foreign students, they may think very little about the extent to which these government policies may be reflected in other venues of the scientific/medical establishment, including the professional hierarchy. They think less or not at all about the absence of women scientists from these positions and why their perspective may be unique and different from that of the men scientists from these countries.

Most scientists also do not notice that scientific contributions and technologies represented in textbooks and lectures find their basis in classical Greece and Rome, presented as part of Western civilization, and that contributions from China, Africa, and Latin America are not acknowledged (Harding, 1998). Modern science is presented as rooted in mechanistic notions arising from Renaissance Europe (Needham, 1969). Since they accept the objectivity of science, science faculty assume that this representation accurately depicts all significant contributions to the history of science and technology, to the extent that they consider the relevance of the history of science at all, given the ahistorical bent to science training and curricula.

READINGS: No readings are necessary here, since this phase develops easily from the curriculum of the current Euro-American educational systems.

Phase II: Recognition that since most scientists are Western/Northern and male, the science they create may reflect a Eurocentric/colonial as well as masculine perspective

For some faculty, the realization that most scientists conducting peer-reviewed research fit the descriptors of Western/Northern and male first hits when they ponder the impact on future generations of scientists and engineers of having the overwhelming majority of graduate students in their field coming from Asia, Africa, and Latin America. In response to Congressional mandates, the National Science Foundation now routinely collects data on the numbers of foreign-born science and engineering students and professionals. Although during the 1980s immigration of scientists and engineers was fairly stable, increasing slightly each year, in 1992 a 62% increase over 1991 occurred in admissions of immigrant scientists and engineers (National Science Board, 1996). The cause appeared to be the Immigration Act of 1990, which permitted large increases in employment-based quotas for highly skilled workers. Despite overall declines in immigration in 1993, the admission of scientists and engineers continued to rise (National Science Board, 1996).

Although few faculty consider the gender ratio of the immigrants, data reveal that women represented 21.3% of scientists and engineers admitted to the United States with permanent resident status in 1993 (National Science Board, 1996). Longitudinal data from 1989 to 1993 show that the number, as well as the proportion, of female scientists and engineers immigrating to the United States increased consistently over time (National Science Board, 1996). Recent immigrant male scientists do not hold key positions in the scientific hierarchy; immigrant female scientists find themselves in even more precarious positions.

Faculty who do recognize that most scientists holding key positions are Western/Northern and male (as well as a few Asian men) may still fail to link the impact that the absence of scientists in general, and women scientists in particular, from developing countries in such positions may have on curriculum and research. Scientific objectivity masks the notion that the research that can be undertaken in today's highly technologically dependent and resource-intensive scientific environment relies heavily on government and foundation funding. Some scientists do not recognize that the overall priorities for research are set by governments. The research priorities of North America and Europe become synonymous with global

priorities and good (fundable) research. Other priorities representing op-
posing alternatives from these mainstream priorities become invisible or
defined as inadequate science. Acceptance of scientific objectivity may
block the question of whether the country of origin, culture, or gender
of a scientist might influence the questions asked, theories, data collected,
or subjects chosen for experimentation, as well as the methods used to
explore those subjects.

READINGS: Chapter 3, "Science and Engineering Workforce" from
Science and Engineering Indicators—1996 (National Science Board, 1996),
particularly the section on "Immigrant Scientists and Engineers," along
with other brief reports produced by the National Science Foundation,
such as *U.S. Science and Engineering in a Changing World*, and the National
Research Council, such as the COSEPUP Report, reveal the U.S. government research and development priorities in science and technology and
their influence on global scientific and technological priorities. Harding's
work, *Whose Science, Whose Knowledge?* (1991), provides a counterpoint to
these statistical articles and points out overlaps in dominance among race,
class, gender, and nationality in scientific theories and priorities.

Phase III: Development of understanding through postcolonial critiques that Eurocentric/Northern, male biases and perspectives may prevent recognition of contributions from other cultures and standpoints

Consideration of the data documenting large numbers of scientists from
Southern continents immigrating to North America and Europe in the
1990s suggests economic and political resources as major, motivating
forces for emigration. The current interest of pharmaceutical companies,
agribusiness, and governments in intellectual property rights in developing countries also suggests attention to the resources and power to be
derived from controlling the science of these countries. Modern scientific
research costs tremendous amounts of money and requires extensive
technological and natural resources. An examination of the history of the
flow of resources between colonizing countries and their colonies provides
a step toward understanding the creation of obstacles that obscure and
devalue some contributions while enhancing and overvaluing others.

As documented by Shiva (1991a), colonialization of India and Africa
by Britain led to a flow of natural resources and labor from the colonies
to support the East India Company, textile mills, and the industrial revolution in Britain in the nineteenth century. This colonial strategy had numerous impacts on both Britain and the colonies: The infusion of resources
from the colony led to accrual of wealth, power, and prestige in the
colonizing country. The colony became de-developed and lost resources,

power, and prestige. The colonizer defined what was valued to its own advantage and to the disadvantage of the colony. Colonial natural resources such as water, forests, and minerals, which had been managed by indigenous organizations for centuries primarily as commons, became commodities managed by the East India Company and colonial rulers. Because of this definition, natural resources from the colony gained considerable added value only after conversion to a product in Britain. Thus, the finished cloth produced in Britain was costly and the final step in its production overvalued, while the cotton, indigo, wood, and other natural resources extracted from India were defined as "raw" and devalued. The skills and labor of the Indian people in maintaining and obtaining the natural resources remained undervalued, while those of the colonial rulers and British capitalists became valued excessively (Shiva, 1991a).

Understanding this history of colonization provides a tool with which to remove some of the obstacles that impede viewing the contributions to science and technology made today by individuals in developing countries. Currently, the pharmaceutical companies remove plants from the rainforest in the developing country and take them to Europe or North America. In the Northern continent the medicinal properties of the plant are extracted, synthesized, and patented to be sold by the pharmaceutical company for an exorbitant profit. Does this de-develop the Southern continent and exploit its resources in a way similar to the British use of India's cotton, indigo, rivers, and forests? Does the current policy of intellectual property rights of ownership by the scientist who splices the gene into the seed, rather than by the women who have cultivated the seed for generations, parallel the undervaluing of the skills and labor of the Indian people who raised the cotton and indigo in the nineteenth century?

READINGS: Writings on postcolonialism and how other disciplines have used postcolonial feminist critiques to broaden their perspectives suggest the richness of these critiques. *Orientalism* by Said (1978) and "Can the Subaltern Speak?" by Spivak (1988) may be especially useful. Readings exploring how colonizing countries viewed the science and technology of the colonies during the period of colonization provide a historical backdrop for understanding current practices such as intellectual property rights in postcolonial situations. Shiva's "The Seed and the Spinning Wheel" (1991b) explores this.

Phase IV: Rediscovery of indigenous science and technology

Knowledge of postcolonial critiques may begin to raise questions about the science and technology obscured in developing countries today. The two-volume work by Bernal, *Black Athena* (Volume 1, 1987; Volume 2,

1991), as well as the seven-volume work by Needham and colleagues (1954), and the work of Weatherford (1988, 1993) begin to uncover the obfuscated histories of science of Africa, China, and Peru, respectively. Some ethnographies by anthropologists provide amazing insights into this issue, as incidental to their accounts of the society.

Ironically, preparatory to their quest for profits to be made from drugs and agribusiness, many of the multinational corporations have sought and found considerable data on indigenous plants and crops. For example, Shiva (1997) states that 75% of the 120 active compounds currently isolated from higher plants and widely used in modern medicine were known in traditional systems. Most others are extracted directly from plants and purified, with less than a dozen coming from synthesis from direct chemical modification. Because the use of traditional knowledge increases the efficiency of pinpointing plants' medicinal uses by over 400%, this results in a thirst for knowledge of indigenous science and technology used to cultivate the crops and harvest the plants.

READINGS: Writings that recover indigenous science and technology and the history of science in ancient non-Western, non-Northern cultures open the door to understanding their contributions and potential new approaches to science and technology. Bernal's introductory chapter in *Black Athena*, Volume I (1987), Needham's "Poverties and Triumphs of the Chinese Scientific Tradition" from *The Grand Titration* (1969), and Weatherford's "Early Andean Experimental Agriculture" from *Indian Givers* (1988) begin this recovery. If read in the absence of an understanding of how this knowledge has been misappropriated and exploited historically and currently, the recovery may fail to introduce ethical dilemmas surrounding indigenous science and technology. Agrawal's "Dismantling the Divide Between Indigenous and Scientific Knowledge" (1995) discusses these dilemmas. Sandra Harding's *Is Science Multicultural?* (1998) details the effects of colonization on science and technology in Southern continents, the extent to which Northern countries used the science and technologies of their colonies to develop their own economies, and the continued colonization of Southern continents through Northern post-World War II development policies, multinational corporations, and globalization.

Phase V: Focus on the current science and technology of developing countries

Postcolonial attitudes have encouraged Western/Northern scientists to devalue the science and technologies of developing countries or to assume that little or no scientific understanding underpins the crops planted and animals bred, forest and river maintenance, or plants used for healing and rituals. These attitudes have led to arrogant assumptions and policies in which agricultural practices or crops successful in Northern continents are seen as the solution to the food crisis in a developing country.

In contrast, Pehu and Rojas (1997) argue that women from developed countries hold biodiversity as the key to new transgenic species and see this as a way to engage the knowledge and participation of women in developing countries in biotechnology:

> The role of community involvement in decision-making and setting the research agenda has been stressed earlier. In many parts of the world, women are the chief managers of natural resources. Today global food security depends on 15 major plant species, while, for example, among the Indians in America it included over 100 species of over 40 genera and 120 families. Much of the selection of resistant maize plants in India is carried out by women. There is remarkable botanical knowledge in rural communities throughout developing countries and there is growing recognition for the role of farm families in in situ conservation of land races and cultivars. (pp. 18–19)

This use of their participation and knowledge for biotechnology development may change the traditional role of such women from keepers and cultivators of seeds for food to producers of sustainable agricultural development for their country.

Rather than assuming that the science and technology of the developing country is either nonexistent, backward, or inappropriate, a postcolonial perspective raises questions about the state of science and technology before colonization, how colonization affected/de-developed the technologies, and whether current practices are the appropriate ones for the environment and culture. Examining the science and technology within the cultural context opens venues for exploring what aspects might be retained and where infusions from Western/Northern science might solve problems.

READINGS: *The Violence of the Green Revolution* (Shiva, 1991b), "After the Forest: AIDS as Ecological Collapse in Thailand" (Usher, 1994), and *The Health of Women: A Global Perspective* (Koblinsky, Timyan, & Gay, 1993) describe some of the problems that have arisen from importation of science and technology from the North without consideration of the science and technology of the Southern country. M. Jacqui Alexander and Chandra Mohanty's *Feminist Genealogies, Colonial Legacies, Democratic Futures* (1997) explores how restructuring of economies in Southern countries parallels privatization in Northern countries, rendering poverty for a larger proportion of people in both developed and developing countries.

Phase VI: Mutually beneficial interchanges and exchanges

Ultimately, it would be desirable to reach a phase where scientists from developing countries in the South and scientists from North America and Europe could share information, science, and technology based on the recognition that each may have much to learn from the other. In this phase, the Northern male scientist would assume the stance of neither the omniscient giver of science and technology nor the exploiter and stealer of seed stocks and medicinal plants from indigenous women. The scientists and technicians from the Southern countries would have the knowledge, resources, and power to evaluate and integrate science and technology from the North in societally appropriate ways. These ways would preserve indigenous knowledge, rights, and communities, while ensuring that the resulting science and technology competed favorably in the global environment.

IMPLICATIONS OF IMPACTS OF TECHNOLOGIES

Globalization, technology, and multinational corporations characterize and unite the Northern, developed and the Southern, developing countries at the beginning of the twenty-first century. Countries of the North serve as the headquarters for most of the technology and multinational corporations, while countries of the South provide raw materials, cheap labor, and markets for the products. Bio- and reproductive technologies follow this pattern, with the developed countries purchasing the seeds from the varieties of plants women have cultivated over generations and genetically engineering them. After gene splicing or other technology has been used to produce monocultures of the crop, which has been made resistant to particular environmental parameters and adapted to agricultural methods in developed countries, the seeds are sold back to the people in the developing world at increased prices. The source of food and the labor of the people, especially of the women, in the developing countries have been devalued. They must pay more for the seeds and accompanying fertilizers and pesticides, and work the land without mechanized help.

In a similar fashion, globalization permits reproductive technologies from developed countries to flow to Southern countries. Often women's bodies become the site of exploitation. For example, in vitro fertilization may be used for a fetus from the union of the sperm and egg of a White,

upper-middle-class man and woman in a developed country to be implanted in the uterus of a poor woman of color from a developing country.
Upon fulfilling the contract to deliver a healthy baby, the woman receives
payment for her labor from the genetic parents, who bring the baby back
to the developed world for rearing.

Postcolonial feminist theories suggest that the globalization and implementation of particular bio- and reproductive technologies vary among
countries because of the particular culture, histories, and geographic and
natural resources of each country. Yet some of the broad implications of
the impacts of these technologies appear relatively clear for women's
work, knowledge, and lives.

First, patents, policies, and constraints used to control these technologies and their applications in the developing countries in ways that hurt
women in these countries will come back to haunt women in the developed world. For example, patent rights and GATT agreements transfer
property ownership of transgenic or genetically engineered species to the
individual who spliced in the new material; although plants cannot be
patented, the individuals who extract the medicinal properties from a
plant that may have been used indigenously for centuries can patent
the extract or its synthetic derivative (Mooney, 1998). Current research
involves the use of remote-sensing technologies to map out medicinal-
plant habitats in Peru (Mooney, 1998). The people who developed the
natural varieties of the seeds or cultivated the herbal plants for generations
often pay exorbitant prices if they wish to grow the genetically altered
seeds and use the herbal plants. Because these policies and trade agreements give control to entrepreneurs, scientists, and corporations, they
have a potentially severe impact on the people, especially women, in
developing countries, who lose control over their natural resources, food,
medicinal-plant sources, and traditional methods of agriculture and healing. This realization led to dramatic public demonstrations in India in
response to W.R. Grace's obtaining U.S. patents on components that can
be used to kill fungi and insects obtained from the neem tree (King &
Stabinsky, 1999).

These same policies, patents, and agreements have begun to rebound
on some segments of the population, including women, of the developed
world. The patent on the BRCA1 and 2 genes threatens to limit access to
research to the few pharmaceutical companies or research institutes capa-
ble of paying for the rights to the license. As a result of restricting the
numbers of researchers and allowing the secrecy that may accompany
work on patented materials, research on cures or treatments for breast
cancer may be slowed and become more costly (see Chapter 2 for a more

complete discussion of this issue). Thus, women in the United States, who through the National Breast Cancer Coalition have protested the patent, may begin to see in patent agreements the common concerns they share with women in developing countries, who potentially may also lose access to their traditional herbal plants.

Second, bio- and reproductive technologies make explicit the connections between the health of the natural environment and the health of people, particularly women. The description by Usher (1994) of the dramatic increase in AIDS in Thailand that resulted from clear-cutting of forest to introduce a genetically engineered species documents this. When this Green Revolution failed, the ravaged environment and reliance on cash crops meant people could no longer produce food. Women, and then young men, entered the sex trade in the cities to raise money to send home to their families who faced worsening economic conditions in the countryside. Malnutrition underpinned the rapid spread of the epidemic of AIDS and other diseases.

A similar environment–health connection is shown by some studies, which remain controversial within the scientific community, of the many environmental pollutants that serve as endocrine disruptor contaminants, such as the classes of dioxins, polychlorinated biphenyls (PCBs), organophosphates, and organochlorides. By acting as biological imposters that mimic estrogen, progesterone, or testosterone, and attaching themselves to appropriate receptors, these disruptors lead to decreases in fertility and birth defects in both animal and human species (Soto et al., 1995). As Guillette (1997) has demonstrated with her studies of Yaqui Indians of Sonora, Mexico, the valley group, exposed to heavy pesticides from farming, experiences higher rates of infertility, spontaneous abortion, premature birth defects, and still births compared with the foothills group, which has lower pesticide exposure. Valley children born without obvious physical defects show lower functional assessment, with decreases in stamina, gross and fine eye–hand coordination, memory, and drawing abilities compared with foothills children. In respects other than pesticide exposure, the two groups shared similar genetics, backgrounds, lifestyles, and sociocultural patterns, with both groups having undergone similar degrees of "modernization" of their customs (Guillette, 1997).

Decreases in human fertility fuel demands for reproductive technologies for those in developed countries who can afford the technologies. Babies born by such technologies in the United States cost in 1996 on the average $16,550–$35,550, depending on region of the country (Lerner, 1996), and will consume 30 times as many of the world's resources as babies in developing countries (Corea, 1991). This consumption places further demands on the environment, which in turn may lead to more use of pesticides, genetically engineered crops, and mechanized agricultural methods.

Third, globalization, technology, and multinational corporations have been, and remain, dominated by men. Men set the agendas, through company ownership and employment, for bringing developing countries into the twenty-first century, for development of technologies, including bio- and reproductive ones, and for the competition of economic capitalism. Male domination means that the impacts of these technologies and developments on women have been ignored or placed outside the central focus. The links between bio- and reproductive technologies, the environment, and women's health require that physicians, scientists, and women's studies scholars with expertise join together to evolve a women-centered critique of current global development and impacts of bio- and reproductive technologies and to set an agenda for future directions. Chapter 4 is devoted to exploring genetics, health, and international development from postcolonial and feminist perspectives to form a basis for such an agenda.

CHAPTER FOUR

Globalization of Bio- and Reproductive Technologies: Opportunities to Enhance or Destroy Women's Work, Knowledge, and Lives

BECAUSE OF MALE DOMINATION of virtually all modern societies, women's studies scholars have pioneered work to bring women into central focus in all disciplines that suffer from exclusion of women's experiences, perspectives, knowledge, and goals. A first step in bringing women from the periphery into the center requires reviewing the history of the field through the lens of women's experience. Such a rereading typically results in an enrichment and transformation of the history of the field. Women's perspectives on events or theories help to recover neglected materials and ideas often overlooked by conventional scholars (Hewitt, 1997). Since the use of bio- and reproductive technologies falls under the confluence of genetics, health, and international development, viewing, at even a superficial level, the history of these fields through the lens of women's experience provides insights into the impacts and applications of bio- and reproductive technologies on women's lives, particularly in developing countries.

A BRIEF LOOK AT GENETICS, HEALTH, AND DEVELOPMENT THROUGH WOMEN'S EYES

Like most scientific disciplines, including biology, genetics has been male-dominated, from the original work of Gregor Mendel and his garden peas in 1865, to his rediscovery in 1900 by Correns, Tschermak, and deVries, to the Drosophila labs of Thomas Hunt Morgan and his colleagues at Columbia University (Starr & Taggart, 1984). Feminist critiques have revealed the extent to which male domination and bias of the field led to the failure to recognize the work of Barbara McClintock on genetic transposition in maize for some 4 decades (Keller, 1983) and to the misappropriation of the crystallography of Rosalind Franklin by Watson and Crick, so crucial to their discovery of the double helical nature of DNA (Sayre, 1975). In addition to recovering the ignored or misunderstood work of women scientists, feminists have questioned whether the reductionism, focus on nuclear control, and use of high technology methods represent male approaches that bias research results against information that might be revealed from study of whole organisms, environmental interactions, and acceptance of a variety of methods that might be more useful in the study of issues of concern to women.

During the latter half of the twentieth century, control mechanisms in simpler organisms began to dominate the research funded and accepted as theoretically valid. One obvious influence on the direction of the research was the phenomenal increase in technologically sophisticated equipment that made it possible to see increasingly smaller structures in simple organisms. Ruth Hubbard (1990) points out the profound influence of the large number of physicists who entered the field of molecular biology, particularly after World War II. Trained as physicists, they transferred some of the tenets of physics—the emphasis on simplicity, deductive reasoning, and the search for universal laws that control—to molecular biology. Despite some growing recognition of the oversimplicity of DNA as the master molecule and its failure to explain data from complex organisms, it continues to dominate the direction of much research in molecular biology.

James Watson, who used Franklin's work to "discover" the double helix (Sayre, 1975), pushed hard for, and served as the first director of, the Human Genome Initiative. His work and this project laid the groundwork for much of the basic research in genetic engineering now applied in bio- and reproductive technologies, suggesting an exclusion of women's priorities from central focus.

In contrast to genetics, women controlled much of traditional health and medicine until the late nineteenth century in most Western countries and until the late twentieth century elsewhere. The history of gynecology has shown a distinct pattern of takeover and control of childbirth and reproductive procedures in the United States by male doctors from female midwives, from the mid-nineteenth century (Ehrenreich & English, 1978; Wertz & Wertz, 1977) to the present time. This history and the more recent history of forced sterilizations (CARASA, 1979), hysterectomies performed too frequently (Centers for Disease Control, 1980), lack of Medicaid funding for abortion, and threatened loss of legal abortion reveal the regulation of women's sexuality and reproduction by the male medical establishment.

Male-dominated medicine and health care relegated women's health to obstetrics/gynecology. Health and disease of the male body became the norm and focus for all other research, diagnoses, and treatment: Women were not included as subjects in experimental trials of drugs; diseases such as cardiovascular disease, affecting both genders, became defined as male diseases, despite mortality and morbidity frequencies in women as high as those in men; and health issues such as incontinence, osteoporosis, and breast cancer, which women reported as important, received minimal funding and study (Rosser, 1994). Partially because of pressure from the women's movement and because of the dawning recognition that lack of baseline data on women's diseases, misdiagnoses, and inappropriate treatments had negative economic consequences for the United States as a whole, as well as causing increased suffering from mortality and morbidity for women, health care practitioners, in defining health, have begun to consider women's experience.

As in genetics and health, male dominance of the field of international development resulted in ignoring and excluding women's work, roles, and knowledge from development policies and their implementation. Northern policies of development have suffered from the assumption that Northern technology, economic policies, and scientific methods that worked in the United States and Europe from the 1860s to the 1970s to transform them from a factory- and agriculture-based economy to an industrial, technical one, would have similar effects in a developing country in the 1980s and 1990s. Given the lack of understanding shown by ignorance of the role that culture, history, geography, climate, timing, and a multitude of other factors played in making these technologies, policies, and methods successful in the North at that particular time, it is not surprising that the men setting the agenda for international development also would ignore the work and experiences of women in developing countries.

In her pioneering book, *Woman's Role in Economic Development*, Ester Boserup (1970) drew attention to the importance of "female systems of farming" and initiated the field of women in development. She demonstrated that female systems of farming were unknown and devalued, despite women's being agricultural wage laborers or the main cultivators on family farms in many parts of the world such as Sub-Saharan Africa, the Caribbean, and Cambodia, Laos, and Thailand, where low population densities, shifting agriculture with hand-held cultivation tools, and few agricultural wage laborers were the norm. In contrast, "male systems of farming" dominated Europe, the Middle East, and North and Latin America, which were characterized by high population densities, capital investment, individual land ownership, settled agriculture, wage laborers, and plows and other machinery. She noted that "European settlers, colonial administrators and technical advisors were largely responsible for the deterioration in the status of women in the agricultural sectors in developing countries" (pp. 53–54) because of assumptions originating from the male systems of farming in which the farmers are male and the women are in the domestic realm (Spring, 1995).

Thinking briefly about the history of genetics, health, and development uncovers the exclusion of women and women's concerns from each field individually; at the confluence of the fields in bio- and reproductive technologies, it is not surprising that women have been far from central, except insofar as they intersect with men's priorities (i.e., use of reproductive technologies to produce children or use of women's knowledge of plants to provide pharmaceutical extracts). How can physicians, scientists, and women's studies scholars rethink these fields and make plans for future directions to empower, rather than destroy, women? This is not an easy task, since rethinking fields involves challenging traditional categories, approaches and methods, what questions are asked and why, and who benefits from the approaches taken.

A MODEL FOR RETHINKING DISCIPLINES

Work by scholars in some areas of women's studies outlines models that have proved useful in rethinking some disciplines. Nancy Hewitt (1997) suggests the following topics for reconceptualizing actors, events, sources, chronologies, and vocabularies in U.S. history to recover women's history: expanding topics, examining diversity, expanding the definition of work, expanding the definition of politics, rethinking major historical events and social movements, and considering women in relation to men. Hewitt's model is similar to the one that I presented in Chapter 3 for including postcolonial perspectives in science curricula in that they both attempt to include perspectives and groups traditionally excluded from study. While Hewitt's model can be applied to curriculum, it also serves as a way of re-visioning a discipline or research field. Perhaps Hewitt's model could serve as a starting place to rethink the basic research and theories underlying bio- and reproductive technologies, health, and international development policies so that they consider and empower women.

Expanding Topics

In academia in general, and in basic scientific research in particular, in the West and North, the applications, usefulness, and beneficiaries of research are separated from its "intrinsic scientific merit," which receives priority and value (Croce, 1995; Hubbard, 1990). Modern geneticists and molecular biologists rely on this notion of objectivity and overlook ways that this separation influences the allocations for funded research. For example, the basic driving force behind the Genome Project is to sequence all of the DNA in the human and many plant and animal species, primarily to obtain basic knowledge; because the project represents basic research, it receives high priority and value.

During early phases of the second wave of feminism, critics of science (Bleier, 1984; Harding, 1986; Hubbard, 1990; Keller, 1985) raised the question of whether practical benefits, usefulness to society, and beneficiaries should be part of decisions to fund and undertake particular scientific research. Recently, the public has begun to raise these issues (Campbell, 1998a) and arrest the progress of major scientific research projects that are perceived as costly relative to their potential significant benefits to society. The response of the Human Genome Project to speed its work because of cheaper, quicker competition from industry (Wheeler, 1998) fuels this perception. The claim by J. Craig Venter and Michael Hunkapiller in May 1998 that they can sequence the human genome more quickly (by 2001 rather than 2005) at a fraction of the cost ($150–$200 million rather than $3 billion) precipitated this response (Campbell, 1998b).

In the United States, Southeast Asia, South America, and Western Europe, the public has opposed life patents and questioned the safety and value of transgenic species, asking whether novel, harmful pathogens such as viruses may be transferred from one species to another (including humans) that have little resistance to them (Wright, 1998). In late summer 1998, Swiss citizens voted for a moratorium on transgenic research; in June 1998 Prince Charles called for a public debate on the merits of allowing genetically engineered food to be grown in Britain ("Prince: Leave Food Making," 1998). Although the European Parliament voted to allow life patents, Italy and the Netherlands attempted to block the move by challenging it in the European Court of Justice (King & Stabinsky, 1999).

From its beginnings, the Human Genome Project set aside small amounts of its budget for ethical, legal, and social implications (ELSI) of the Project. In the wake of current controversies, more of the Human Genome Project budget has been earmarked for ELSI. This increase stems from growing questions about diversion of limited resources from public health programs proven to decrease mortality and morbidity, especially for women and children through vaccinations, improved sanitation, and nutrition, to high tech research for gene sequencing with little proven direct impact on health. Although the nonscience-oriented public may have quite different theoretical and political bases than feminists for requiring more attention to social impacts, health benefits, and economic costs/benefits for basic research, the current agendas and questions of both groups coincide in their requests for accountability to society.

From the beginnings of the second wave of the women's movement in the 1960s, feminists also have sought major reform in health care, calling attention to exclusion of women and for a focus on women's health. Many groups, including the American College of Obstetricians and Gynecologists and the American College of Women's Health Physicians, seek to expand the definition of women's health. Even the public supports feminist physicians in requests to end the bifurcation of medical specialties that resulted in women's health being synonymous with obstetrics/gynecology.

Women's health moves women from the periphery to the central focus for all aspects of medical research, diagnosis, treatment, and access to health care. Expanding beyond the traditional limits of reproductive issues such as pregnancy, childbirth, menopause, ovarian hormones, menstrual cycles, contraception, and use of reproductive technologies, women's health also includes differences in frequency, symptoms, and effects of diseases found in both sexes. Such differences occur in cardiovascular diseases, many lung diseases (such as primary pulmonary hypertension), sexually transmitted diseases, gastrointestinal disorders (such as gallstones), neurological disorders (such as multiple sclerosis and migraine headaches), urinary tract disorders (such as incontinence), and psychiatric and behavioral problems (such as depression, anxiety, and eating disorders). Women's health encompasses sex differences at the molecular level in metabolism of drugs, including their interactions with hormones; exposure to environmental toxins; and absorption of food, vitamins, and minerals. This expanded definition extends throughout women's life span from before adolescence through aging, including end-of-life issues and dying; it encompasses all facets of women's life, recognizing that sociocultural issues such as domestic violence, rape, child abuse, and poverty are primary health issues for women and their families.

International development has tended to exclude women, despite their role as chief manager of natural resources in many parts of the world. In India, for example, much of the selection of resistant maize plants is carried out by women. Spring (1995) documents studies showing that African women contribute from 30–80% of the labor and management in food production and lesser amounts in cash crop production and livestock, and that a third of African rural households are headed by women who perform most of the farmwork with the aid of their children.

Failures of some development policies because of lack of understanding of the crucial role women play in farming, resource management, or food production have led to some recognition of the need to focus on gender and women in formulating policies. Spring (1995) discusses lessons learned from research and development activities with women in Africa, particularly Malawi. Recognized national policies that take into account women's reproductive, productive, and community functions, and legal access to land and resources, form crucial components needed for success. Likelihood for success is enhanced when practitioners, bureaucrats, and decision makers influential in these projects receive appropriate gender-analysis training regarding women in development. Pehu and Rojas (1997), as suggested in Chapter 3, call for participatory approaches and multidisciplinarity in biotechnology research and applications as ways to include women since "it seems that the scientific community suffers from 'inbreeding' and lacks experience from other institutional and disciplinary backgrounds and the life experience of female and ethnic minority scientists" (p. 19).

Bio- and reproductive technologies cross disciplinary boundaries and require participation of the scientific community, the multinational corporations for funding and implementation, and the public, particularly women, of both developed and developing countries. Each discipline and its practitioners need to expand the definition of topics they consider central to consider the variety of issues crucial to the interdisciplinary questions surrounding biotechnologies.

Examining the Complexity of Diversity

Attempts to reread the history of these fields through the lens of women's perspectives and to expand topics constitute the first and second steps toward including women. Once women become a central focus, the diversity that race/ethnicity, class, gender, sexual orientation, age, and nationality bring to women's lives increases the necessary complexity with which issues need to be analyzed to avoid oversimplification of the uses and abuses of bio- and reproductive technologies.

Some of the ethical and social issues raised by the research and sequence results from the HGP may be seen quite differently and have varied impacts on women's lives, depending on where women live and who they are. For example, White, middle-class feminists in the North, as well as anthropologists and ethicists, lobbied for the Human Genome Diversity Project (HGDP), partially because of their sensitization to issues of inclusion. Because of the history of exclusion of men of color and women from clinical drug trials (Campbell, 1998c; U.S. General Accounting Office, 1990), they thought that diversity, particularly racial/ethnic diversity, should be a component of such basic research. In contrast, some individuals, including women, from the ethnic populations, especially the so-called vanishing populations, questioned whether the Diversity Project stood as a potential step toward genocide. Did sequencing their genes mean that the people themselves would become expendable?

The implementation and use of reproductive technologies demonstrate quite vividly the significance of diversity among women surrounding health issues. As suggested in the discussion of socialist-feminist and postcolonial-feminist theories in Chapter 2, the use of low technology techniques such as cesarean section and higher tech processes such as in vitro fertilization and rented uteri varies within countries and among countries. Pressures to make women conform to the norms of the patriarchal culture and class within which they are located provide similarities for women in the use of these technologies. Different cultures, classes, races, and nationalities provide the parameters for differences of use between women within a culture and among cultures.

Although differences and complexities among cultures represent one type of diversity, class differences represent another. Women in developed countries experience more use of such technologies than women in developing countries, possibly because of socioeconomic differences between less- and more-developed countries. Sometimes class serves as the most reliable predictor of the use of technologies on women across cultures. Substantial abuses resulting from the refusal to remove Norplant in Bangladesh, first revealed in the 1980s, continue in 1998 (Gillespie, 1998). Because of government policies seeking to decrease fertility, health practitioners refuse to remove the Norplant transdermal sticks when women complain of side effects ranging from continual bleeding, through migraines and dizziness, to ectopic pregnancies. Similar coercion occurs in U.S. inner cities, where Norplant is implanted in welfare mothers, primarily African Americans, as a condition for receipt of checks, and in Native American women who receive health care from the Indian Health Service on reservations (Washburn, 1996).

In international development, policies often have failed because of inabilities to appreciate the complexities of biodiversity, geographic diversity, and cultural diversity both among and within countries. The decrease in biodiversity in developing countries caused by the use of farm methods from the U.S. midwest, which depend on large fields of monocultures, illustrates failures to recognize complexities between countries surrounding these diversities. In the volume, *The Tree Against Hunger*, Brandt and colleagues (1997) suggest that within Ethiopia, similar failures to recognize diversities may prevent some regions from using enset as a food crop, even during extreme famine. For example, although some farmers in Lalibela grow a few enset plants near their houses to use the leaves to bake bread in, they have no knowledge of its use as a food. This area of northern Ethiopia lost thousands of people to famine in the mid-1980s; use of enset as food has been restricted to the southern highland region (Brandt et al., 1997).

The enset-based agricultural systems in Ethiopia also reveal diversities with regard to culture regarding factors such as urban–rural, class, and gender differences within a single country. While unheard of as a food in some parts of Ethiopia, in other parts, enset has been perceived as "peasant food." Brandt and colleagues (1997) report that "there has been a breakdown in the cultural perception of enset food products as peasant food" (p. 49), which has led to its being bought in markets and consumed in restaurants in Addis Ababa.

Brandt and colleagues (1997) report diversity of enset cultivation and processing based on ethnicity, gender, and class of Ethiopians:

> Between ethnic groups where enset is a staple (Gurage and Sidama) and a co-staple for some of the population (the wealthier households among the Hadiya) there are differences in many aspects of enset cultivation (clonal variation, plant spacing, disease prevalence, and manuring) and processing (tools and starter used, location, size, and disease of pits). The gender division of labor varies between groups and households, and there are differences in the mix of farm, off-farm, and non-farm enterprises (p. 38).

> Wealthier households have greater clonal variation, as well as having more mature and a larger number of enset plants. . . . Women in wealthier households reduce the drudgery of enset processing by hiring labor. Poor women have the double burden of working and processing on their own farms and selling their labor for such tasks to wealthier households. (p. 39)

Gender remains a constant that unites women across differences of race, class, age, ability, and sexualities within and among cultures. Bio- and reproductive technologies have widely varying uses, impacts, and perceptions, which depend partially on the complexities of these differences.

Expanding the Definition of Work

The example of enset reveals more than the importance of recognizing the complexity of diversity on a variety of levels. It also suggests the salience of expanding the definition of work to ensure that women's roles receive recognition and to recognize the variance of gender roles among cultures and different roles assumed by women in the same culture.

Balancing work/family issues has become a "hot topic" in the United States recently (Radcliffe Public Policy Institute, 1996). Books, conferences, and government task forces now focus on the subject. Much of the need to balance comes from the organization of work and family predominating in the mid-twentieth-century United States. The model assumed a male breadwinner who left home to earn money from outside in the market economy; the woman stayed at home and took care of the family. Although this Ozzie and Harriet model probably never fit most American families, today in two-thirds of married American couples both the husband and wife are in the workforce, up from 42% in 1975 (Herz & Wooten, 1996). In 1992, 69.4% of employed mothers with children under the age of 3 worked full time (Costello & Stone, 1994). One of the numerous problems and misconceptions of this model was its failure to count what women did in the home as work. Childcare, eldercare, and housework were defined as outside the gross national product; these did not count as work. Ironically, with 72% of mothers in the paid workforce (Jones, 1998), women's working outside the home and fitting the male definition of work have revealed some of the "work" assumed by women inside the home. The childcare, housework, and community service "nonwork" performed by women becomes redefined as "work" when it must be purchased, assumed by men, or left undone.

In a similar fashion, women's work in genetics research, health, and development needs to be recognized and defined. Earlier in this chapter, I alluded to the ignoring, misunderstanding, and misappropriation of the work of women geneticists such as Rosalind Franklin and Barbara McClintock. Today, the work of people as geneticists in developing countries has been ignored. Although these people, often the women, have bred the lines producing the varieties of seeds and cultivars to produce transgenic species, Northern scientists and entrepreneurs ignore their work and/or define it as nonscience. As Harding (1998) points out, much of the science and technology produced by people in Southern continents does not count as science. Because these women do not know the vocabulary of genetics, do not use high technology methods such as gene sequencing, and use the fields of nature rather than laboratories to grow their seeds, their contributions are not defined as work, science, or genetics.

Yet their knowledge of interbreeding plants, maintenance of biodiversity, soil and weather conditions, natural pesticides, and ecological resource management has sustained their families for centuries. Recognition of indigenous science emerged as a central issue for women at the 1995 Beijing Conference. Schooled in high technology definitions of work and science, dependent on words such as DNA, computer sequencing, and retroviruses, women from Northern, industrialized countries lagged in accepting indigenous women's contributions in this arena as work and science.

Not only have the contributions of women geneticists, such as Franklin and McClintock, been overlooked and ignored, but women's genetic and biological contributions historically have been misunderstood and marginalized, often resulting in wrong scientific theories. In ancient Greece, for example, women were believed to be colder than men (and therefore less developed) and to provide only nutritive value for the developing fetus; the form and motion were believed to come from the male only (Tuana, 1989). This theory, included in the notion of preformationism, in which the sperm contained a homunculus (a completely formed individual) that grew via the nutrition provided by the egg, influenced biology for centuries. When Van Leeuwnehoek looked through the microscope he invented, he claimed to observe two kinds of spermatozoa, one from which the male developed and the other from which the female developed (Tuana, 1989). Masculine and feminine social roles may have subtly pervaded other theories of development. As recently as 1989, the Biology and Gender Study Group pointed out that theories about the relationship between the nucleus and the cytoplasm within the cell were patterned on husband–wife interactions within the nuclear family. The issue was who had control—the husband (nucleus) or wife (cytoplasm):

> The nucleus came to be seen as the masculine ruler of the cell, the stable yet dynamic inheritance from former generations, the unmoved mover, the mind of the cell. The cytoplasm became the feminine body of the cell, the fluid, changeable, changing partner of the marriage. (Biology and Gender Study Group, 1989, p. 179)

Not only does the nucleus/husband and cytoplasm/wife analogy demonstrate the influence of gender on scientific theories, it also illustrates the search for reductionism to a simpler or single part that controls and directs other differentiation.

In its focus on gene sequencing and DNA, the Human Genome Initiative again centers on the importance of genes, the portion that males and females contribute equally to the next generation. This focus downplays the role of the surrounding environment and environmental–genetic inter-actions, the milieu for development contributed solely by the female. Despite increasing evidence of environment as a mediator of genetic expression, genetic transposition as explored by McClintock, and the com-plexity of higher organisms, the spotlight remains on genes.

In contrast, scientists develop the overwhelming number of reproduc-tive technologies for use on women's bodies. The contribution by the male of either an X or a Y chromosome determines the genetic sex of the offspring. Yet, women must undergo amniocentesis for sex determination. When an unwanted female child is determined, the woman must bear the abortion. Men bear responsibility for at least half of the causes of infertility; yet almost all infertility treatments, with the exception of sperm tests, represent reproductive technologies (e.g., IVF, artificial insemina-tion) developed for use on women's bodies. Although reproduction clearly has been defined as women's work, this work has limits that benefit male control. Men's work has been defined as the genetic contribution of the sperm. In a legal decision, a California judge ruled that the woman who provided the egg, not the woman gestating the fetus, is the biological mother (Hubbard, 1995), thereby using the male norm of genetic contribu-tion to define biological motherhood in women. Men's work also includes development and use of reproductive technologies to control procreation. Feminists have critiqued the conversion of the normal, natural process of pregnancy, labor, and childbirth controlled by women into a clinical, often surgical procedure controlled by men (Ehrenreich & English, 1978; Holmes, 1981). They also have warned of the extent to which reproductive technologies place pressure on women to produce the "perfect" child, while placing control in the hands of the male medical establishment.

Just as indigenous women's maintenance of natural resources and seeds was defined as nonwork, partially because of its perception as nonscience, women's knowledge of disease and maintenance of health in the family and community also have been defined as nonwork and nonscience in both developed and developing countries. Using observa-tion, trial and error, and sharing of information across generations, women used methods of cleaning and cooking and fed their families food to maximize health and minimize disease; women learned which plants held medicinal properties. Part of their indigenous scientific knowledge included recognition of herbal remedies to enhance fertility, prevent con-ception, and cause abortion. The major efforts made by pharmaceutical companies to identify the plants used in traditional healing in indigenous cultures today constitutes some recognition of the women's knowledge. However, just as when doctors obtained herbal remedies from midwives and witches in the nineteenth century in the United States (Ehrenreich &

English, 1978), the modern pharmaceutical companies award the patent to the scientist who does the "work" of synthesizing the compound based on the extract from the medicinal plant, thereby defining the indigenous women's knowledge as nonscience and as nonwork.

Since the United States and other Northern countries fail to recognize and count women's work unless it is performed outside the home in the public sphere, their transfer of this failure to other countries when developing and implementing models for international development reflects both ethnocentric and androcentric biases. As discussed earlier in this chapter, Boserup (1970) revealed that individuals conceiving such models assumed not only that what worked to develop the North American and European economies would be successful in an entirely different culture in the mid-twentieth century, but also that women in the cultures of developing countries performed similar roles to those of women in Northern, developed countries. Since they ignored the work done by Northern women, except for that done outside the home in the public sphere for wages, they also failed to recognize the work of women in developing countries. Boserup (1970) discussed the overlooking of the importance of women's labor and responsibilities in agriculture because of the developmental emphasis on extractive crops. She also documented women's systematic deprivation of land rights through new laws and regulations negating women's prior rights and development-originated land reforms that transferred land holdings to husbands as heads of households.

Sondra Hale (1998), in her work on Sudanese women, discusses ways in which women's work in the informal sector does not "count." Because many of their economic activities are carried out at or near their residences or in the homes of others, the work of Sudanese women as brewers, street vendors, tailors, basket makers, weavers, potters, needleworkers, domestic servants, midwives, wedding ritual/ceremonial specialists, spiritual experts, healers, ritual mediators, musician/singers, beauticians, shopkeepers, bartenders, prostitutes, and market merchants has not been enumerated in the census as work. Because a number of these jobs are cottage industries performed at home, in private, or in a closed neighborhood setting, payment is often in kind or in goods, although many earn irregular wages for this work (Hale, 1998).

This failure to understand women's work and contributions, coupled with imposition of Northern assumptions of males as "head of household," often deprived women of their land in agrarian reform and land tenancy. As Jean Davison's (1988) work reveals, in Africa, women in patrilineal societies typically worked the land of their husbands without having the right to inherit property and with occasional rights to allocate

the results of production; in contrast, African women in matrilineal societies received land through their kin and also might cultivate some of
their husband's fields. Cultivation of cash crops and creation of land
commodities altered gender relations in terms of decision making:

> Lack of power to make intra-family decisions about how land and crops are
> allocated or to make decisions about the allocation of income from cash crop
> production, has led many women to seek extra-family means of generating
> income to purchase commodities . . . or to purchase additional land. (Davi-
> son, 1988, p. 14)

In sum, women's knowledge of seeds and cultivars and of medicinal
plants stands as central information for many biotechnology innovations
in transgenic crops and extractions for pharmaceutical properties. Wom-
en's bodies serve as the site where most reproductive technologies are
developed, tested, and applied. Simultaneously, these contributions of
women have been defined as nonscience and nonwork. Redefining work
to include women's roles may change the perspectives on these technologies.

Redefining Politics

Public/private bifurcations that defined men's work—performed outside
the home, recognized and counted—from women's work—performed
inside the home, unrecognized and uncounted—also underpin definitions
of politics. With the exception of some of the Scandinavian countries
(Faludi, 1996), women in Northern/Western industrialized countries lack
substantial representation in the political hierarchy. The United States has
never had a woman president, and as of 1998, women held 11% (65) of
congressional seats (Hales, 1998); at the state level, women represented
25.4% of statewide elected officials, 21.5% of state legislators, and 22.0%
of highest-court justices, with significant state by state variance (Center
for Women in Government, 1998). Policies and funds legislated and exe-
cuted at the federal level set the parameters and have primary influence on
basic genetic research, health, and international development. Women's
absence at this level means that much of politics is defined without women
and excludes women's concerns.

Redefining politics to include women involves consideration of social
movements, including grassroots organizations, cooperatives, support
groups, and networks. Early feminist critiques of genetic research (Bleier,
1984; Hubbard, 1979, 1983) emerged from consciousness-raising groups
and women's studies, the academic arm of the women's movement in the

late 1960s. More recent critiques directed specifically at the HGI (Fausto-Sterling, 1992; Holmes, 1998; Hubbard, 1990, 1995; Rosser, 1997b, 1998) built on work of the earlier feminist critics who raised questions about reductionism, social responsibility, allocation of resources, and effects on marginalized, nondominant groups. Coalitions and networks, encompassing groups such as disability rights groups, people of color, and ethicists who share overlapping concerns about the HGI, have obtained some of the ELSI funds from the HGP to hold conferences such as the one in 1996 on feminist critiques of the HGI (Holmes, 1996).

The women's health movement in the United States and globally has had gradually increasing influence on the formal, federal political processes to obtain more resources and access to create research, policy, and processes benefiting women's health. Women's health became national news in the 1970s through efforts of the women's movement, including the efforts of the Boston Women's Health Book Collective with the publication of the first edition of their now classic book, *Our Bodies, Ourselves* (1973), which increased women's knowledge of their own bodies and health. In 1985, the U.S. Public Health Service surveyed the nation and recommended changes in the national approach to women's health by expanding the definition beyond reproductive health. After the report by the General Accounting Office (GAO) that the National Institutes of Health expended only 13.5% of its budget on women's health issues, and that the majority of studies on issues affecting both men and women had inadequate representation of women as subjects (Sagraves, 1995), the Congressional Caucus for Women's Issues introduced the Women's Health Equity Act in 1990. In 1991, Bernadine Healy, M.D., the first woman director of the National Institutes of Health, established the Office of Research on Women's Health, with Vivian W. Pinn, M.D., as its first director. The Women's Health Initiative, the largest longitudinal, comprehensive, community-based study, including 40 sites for data collection, on the impact of clinical intervention and prevention in women's health, was announced by that office in 1991. The Public Health Service Office on Women's Health was established in 1991, followed by offices or positions concerned with women's health issues at agencies within the federal government. The Office of Research on Women's Health held its First Annual Congress on Women's Health in 1992. Partnering women's health research, education, clinical care, and community services, the first six model Centers of Excellence in Women's Health were funded in 1996 by the Department of Health and Human Services. Increasing numbers of medical schools have established or expanded curricula on women's health, as have institutions that prepare individuals for other health professions, including dentistry, nursing, and allied health professions. Current efforts center on development of clinical competencies, residencies, and public policy focused on women's health and health care delivery.

The coalitions of women's support groups, organizations, and networks have documented the benefits of research on women's health to all of society (healthier women give birth to healthier children, both male and female) and the costs of inadequate attention (misdiagnosis of heart attacks, higher death rates from bypass and angioplasty, and lack of understanding of effects of myocardial infarction medication due to research on males only). This documentation leads to more interaction of women with the formal political process; politics becomes broadened and redefined slightly to include some women and some of women's health concerns.

As the results of the 1991 National Council for International Health Conference on Women's Health: The Action Agenda (Koblinsky, Timyan, & Gay, 1993) and the 1995 Beijing Conference (Basch, 1996) underline, poverty causes two-thirds of the world's women to have poor health. As Jacobson (1993) reports:

> Common symptoms of this fast-spreading ailment include chronic anemia, malnutrition, and severe fatigue. Sufferers exhibit an increased susceptibility to infections of the respiratory and reproductive tracts. And premature death is a frequent outcome. (p. 3)

Six of the twelve items of a list of "What We Want—Voices from the South" focus on health, contraception, and family planning issues (Jacobson, 1993). UNICEF reported at the Beijing Conference that 585,000 women die each year in pregnancy or childbirth, mostly from preventable or treatable problems (Moses, 1995). Where men and women receive equal access to resources and health care, there are about 106 females for every 100 males. "In China and South and West Asia, there are only 94 females for every 100 males. In China, some 49 million women appear to be 'missing.' Worldwide, approximately 100 million women are missing" (Antrobus, 1995, p. 6). By linking reproductive rights to human rights, women from widely varying national, cultural, and religious backgrounds reached consensus on a reproductive rights platform:

> The human rights of women include their right to have control over and decide freely and responsibly on matters related to their sexuality, including sexual and reproductive health, free of coercion, discrimination and violence. (Basch, 1996, p. 41)

This platform led to some positive benefits in South Africa, Argentina, Ukraine, and Poland. These international coalitions provide limited help in the continued resistance to "recognizing the special health and reproductive issues of women" (Basch, 1996, p. 42).

As an extension and product of the politics of Northern countries, policies of international development have ignored women's contributions to politics in Southern countries unless they fit the mold of publicly elected office. Women's political power in the tribe, community, church, or women's groups appeared invisible since it failed to conform to the mold of elected office in the public sphere.

Sondra Hale (1998) describes the extent to which women's networks and organizations in the Sudan remain unrecognized, even by some progressive women leaders:

> A special section of the market which women totally controlled and regulated, existed in Omdurman until recently. These women were often economically autonomous and extended this autonomy into the domestic sphere. They were able to do this through the collective power they had built within their various kin networks as an extension of their workplace. In my interviews with progressive women leaders, I heard much discussion about the need to create cooperatives for women, but no mention of the fact that these already existed. There was no mention of extant neighborhood collectives and the possibility of building onto them or imitating their organizing strategies. Nor did I hear any recognition of the need to devise strategies for organizing among women students through their daily lives in the hostel. (n.p.)

Limited progress has emerged from the failure of some development projects due to lack of understanding that women played a critical role in success of the project. For example, Spring (1995) discusses malnutrition, especially in children, which resulted when the importance of women's contribution to feeding rural families was underestimated by development projects supporting commercial crop production:

> A classic example concerned cocoa production in Ghana when men, assisted by women, began growing this new cash crop (Bukh, 1979). Subsequently, the staple yam crop became more and more women's responsibility because the men were busy with the cocoa. The women had an increased workload, and over the years shifted from growing yams to cassava that required less labor expenditure. However, cassava was less nutritious, depleted the soil more quickly and was less capable of being intercropped. (p. 18)

In contrast, Harding (1998) suggests that planners may have understood very well what they were doing and how they used women in
development projects:

> Development policies were destroying the environments and cultures of the
> "unaligned nations" that had become the "Third World" during the Cold
> War period. Women were not at all left out of the narrow, economistic,
> development planning of the early postwar years, as a series of such postcolo-
> nial accounts countered. The appropriation of women's labor, land rights,
> and natural resources has been a crucial generator of profit for elites in
> the North and their allies in the south over the entire last half century of
> development policy. (pp. 80–81)

In some cases, women have organized to stop projects in development
that they view as detrimental to their families, communities, and countries.
The women of Chipko prevented destruction of the forest for commercial
exploitation and consequent instability in the surrounding Himalayan
villages (Shiva, 1989). Their tree hugging not only saved the environment,
challenging the reductionist commercial forestry system, but it also questioned the financial greed and alcoholism of the local men who had begun
to cooperate with the Forest Development Corporation to obtain cash
(Shiva, 1989).

Both the African and Indian (Chipko) examples demonstrate a misunderstanding of women's political clout/organization and/or a translation
of Northern ideas of male-dominated political power to Southern nations.
Redefining politics to include women typically means examining groups
outside of the official, elected power hierarchy. Women's political power
often resides in the social movements of grassroots organizations, cooperatives, support groups, and networks rather than in the executive, legisla-
tive, and judicial bodies both in Northern and Southern countries.

Rethinking Major Historical Events, Social Movements, and Gender Relationships

Redefining politics to include women frequently results in rethinking and
re-viewing historical events and movements and the roles that men and
women played in those events. When the focus shifts from the dominant
group with power, different events, movements, and relationships may
appear significant. In their views of an event, women often share a perspective more like that of men of their own community than of women
of other communities.

The dominant group of scientists and male politicians appears to
mark the progress of modern genetics with a series of historical events

that explore the question, What is life? by reductionism and control of life at the level of the gene. The discovery by Watson and Crick of the double-helical nature of DNA and its base pairs, which make up the universal genetic sequence for all organisms (Watson, 1969), stands as a major event. The "central dogma" of hierarchy, where unidirectional flow from DNA in the nucleus to messenger RNA to protein in the cytoplasm dictates life processes, emphasized nuclear control. The Human Genome Project, founded by Watson, who served as its first director, constitutes the major event now in process. Reductionism and control in the form of DNA as the master molecule underlie the foundations of the Human Genome Project.

Feminist scientists and others outside the dominant group might have a different perspective on the significant events in this history. In addition to noticing the failure to recognize the substantial contribution of Rosalind Franklin to the discovery of the double-helical nature of DNA and her shameful treatment by Watson and Crick, they might remark that the notion of trying to find out "what is life" by breaking down living organisms to small chemical units, may be excessively reductionistic. They would realize that early on, Barbara McClintock's work revealed that information flow was not unidirectional, that genes "jumped around," and that a much more interactive model fit the data from higher organisms much better than did the unidirectional Watson–Crick model. Currently, they have worked to raise questions about the proliferation and release of transgenic species. They critique the spending of billions of federal dollars for the HGP as a questionable use of resources, particularly in a time of tight fiscal constraints. They point out that the HGP is reductionistic and controlling in that it isolates the gene (not even the gene interaction with the environment) as the focus for disease. This is problematic in that genetic defects are responsible for only a small percentage of diseases. Even for those diseases, such as cancer and cardiovascular disease, that have a genetic component, it is the interaction of those genetic components with environmental factors that determines who gets the disease. Most disease and death in our society are not due to genetic defects. Poverty, malnutrition, lack of education about prevention, and lack of access to existing medical care such as vaccination and prenatal care are the major causes of disease and death. By focusing on sequencing DNA in chromosomes, the HGP diverts money from known cures for disease. It suggests a simple biological basis for problems that have complex social and economic causes in our society.

Feminist critics purporting this view have been joined by some men who share their perspective. Many of these men come from outside the dominant group. Race, class, sexual orientation, ability status, or other factors make them representative of groups likely to experience the impact of the Human Genome Project in unique ways. Their differences from the White, middle- to upper-class male scientist most closely identified with the HGP may serve as the basis for their forming a coalition with feminists who critique the project. For others, Marxist, African American, or other political/theoretical positions stand at the origin of their overlap with feminist concerns about the project. Heeding the lessons learned from the use of amniocentesis and tests available for AIDS and sickle cell anemia, which have made people of color and people of lower socioeconomic status particularly vulnerable to applications from genetic testing, these men understand the need for safeguards to protect homosexuals, women, the disabled, and people of color from some negative effects of the application of human genome mapping.

Significant events in recent health care history also may be viewed differently by women, compared with men from the dominant group serving as physicians. The traditional history of medicine dates the Flexner Report (1910) as a significant event that marked the modern era of medicine and medical training. This influential report espoused a medical training model involving 2 years of basic science education followed by 2 years of clinical education and inpatient hospital and outpatient clinic settings to produce a physician who is an autonomous separate authority. This report resulted in the closure of irregular medical schools (including those admitting women and healers); established medicine as a science, based in experimentation, germ theories, and objectivity; and focused on individual patients with acute medical and surgical problems and on technological approaches to those problems. Based on criteria established by the report, other events, such as antibiotics, double-blind placebo experiments, and compartmentalization of knowledge into demarcated specialties, have led to progress in decreasing mortality and morbidity caused by microorganisms and anatomical causes that led to early death and shortened life span. The new improvements in technology, understanding of genetic causes of disease, and possibilities of genetic engineering are seen as keys to eradication of modern diseases—cancer, cardiovascular disease, and AIDS.

Feminists (Altekruse & Rosser, 1992; Morantz-Sanchez, 1988) have critiqued this view of medical history and progress. They have noted that the Flexner Report established the hierarchy, authority, and control of the White male physician who displaced midwives, irregular physicians, and others with alternative approaches to healing. Feminists note that much of the decrease in mortality and morbidity came from advances in public health through vaccination and sanitation, rather than through advances in medicine. Feminists (Dan, 1994; Fee, 1982; Rosser, 1994) have revealed that often the "objective" and so-called value-free medical research suffered from the biases of the gender, race, and class held by researchers and practitioners, who were overwhelmingly male, White, and upper class. Dominance of the male physician within the profession led to androcentrism in research; viewing the male as the norm resulted not only in exclusion of women as subjects in experimental and clinical trials, but also in the trivialization and denial of women's objective symptoms by medical practitioners. Increasing specialization has led to the United States having the highest medical costs in the world and to inappropriate and inadequate approaches to many women's health issues that are determined by the interaction of economic, political, and social forces, as well as biological factors that do not fit well into any specialty (e.g., breast cancer) (Rosser, 1994). Feminists warn that new technologies, genetic causes of disease, and genetic engineering may hurt, rather than advance, women's health. They suggest that the current system's gaps between the haves and have nots are likely to result in the rich having access to such technologies, as well as gene enhancement and gene therapy to improve their intelligence, health, and physical traits; the negative impacts, such as if, and when, an abortion should occur if a fetus has a genetic condition that may result in a disability, are likely to fall disproportionately on women.

Again, many men who see the shortcomings of the current health care system, in which access depends on class, gender, race, sexual orientation, and ability status, have joined feminists in similar critiques. In some cases, such as male homosexual activists' fight for AIDS research and funding, males have provided useful models and coalitions for feminists and advocates of women's health. Many men have joined feminists in agreeing that universal health care coverage and separation of health insurance from employment stand as crucial steps to remedy the situation for women and most men.

Women, especially women from developing countries, typically see the significant events in the history of international development differently from the men, especially men from developed countries, who formulate and implement policies. During the 1980s, a worsening economic crisis brought a decline in per-capita income, balance-of-payments problems, deteriorating terms of trade, and heavy debt burdens for developing countries. This left a growing number of households unable to meet their basic needs. Government investments vital to women shrank, while the number of female-headed households multiplied; the combination of increased family responsibilities and diminished economic prospects combined to force women to engage in a perilous balancing act to support themselves and their families. "Adjustment programs were designed without consideration of their impact on human conditions. . . . As a result, they have damaged the human and capital resource base available to society" (Agrawal et al., 1995, p. 437). Basically, such programs are the product of development strategies based on "indicators of progress" that systematically fail to account for women's social and economic contributions to society (Jacobson, 1993, p. 8).

Rethinking major historical events and social movements in genetics, health, and international development from the perspective of women reveals different views of success, progress, and failure. Men have dominated and controlled these events and movements, usually to women's detriment, in all arenas. Because of their race, class, gender, sexual orientation, nationality, or other factors, some men share views of the events and visions of the future that are more similar to those of most women than to those of the men in control; a few women share the view of the dominant men. The history of each field demonstrates struggles for power and control of agendas, resources, and leadership. Although the dominant group usually has control, women, particularly when they join in coalitions with groups who share concerns on particular issues, can influence and sometimes implement their agendas. Struggle characterizes the process and results.

This rethinking suggests that for globalization of bio- and reproductive technologies, women physicians, scientists, and scholars in women's studies should form coalitions. Uniting furthers the chances that these technologies will become opportunities to enhance rather than destroy women's knowledge, work, and lives.

Fusion of Practice and Theory:
Tales from Three Continents

THEORIES PROVIDE SIGNIFICANT frameworks for understanding the implications of technologies and their impacts. Understanding how theories and technologies play out in practice requires that lenses be refocused from the more distanced, big picture to the daily lives of people up close. During three professional and personal international trips, I had opportunities to consider interactions between science, scientists, and women in three rather different cultures.

THE POLITICAL IS PERSONAL: EFFECTS ON
DAILY LIVES OF WOMEN AND SCIENCE

These three international experiences within a 3-month period in Kenya, Canada, and Sweden brought home to me the salience and urgency of coalition formation. These experiences also gave me new ideas about several aspects of feminism and postcolonial critiques. They provided insights into U.S. science education and research agendas that I previously had naively assumed to be divorced from postcolonial critiques.

Science Education in Postcolonial Kenya

I went to Africa to see the animals and visit my younger college-aged daughter. One of the reasons I wanted to see Kenya at that time was because of the rapid rate of disappearance of species each year, largely the result of neocolonial ideas of development that cause destruction of species' habitats, partially to obtain resources for the developed world. For example, current estimates suggest we are losing one species of life each day from the tropical forests (Shiva, 1989). Not this information, but my daughter's descriptions of teaching math and science to high school students in a small village near Kakamega in the western part of Kenya, provided the first awakenings of how postcolonial critiques might apply to the United States. She discussed the discrepancies between the requirements of the Kenyan curriculum (adopted from the model of the British colonizer's curriculum) as translated into the expectations required by the national examinations students must pass and the realities of the everyday classroom situation. These included no laboratory equipment, overcrowded classes, underprepared teachers, and the assumption that memorization passed for understanding. The lingering colonial presence of Britain and its resulting failure to permit the flowering of structures most appropriate for the education of Kenyan people became symbolized for her in the required daily flag-raising and saluting ceremony in the absence of a flag and pole.

A visit to the Kenyan National Museum in Nairobi provided the second insight. Because of its focus on natural history, the museum houses many of the original Australopithecus and *Homo erectus* fossils, including *Australopithecus afarensis*, the famous Lucy, found by Johanson, the Leakeys, and co-workers. Knowing this, I was shocked when we first began to explore the rooms in the museum. The guidebook's statements about the inferior maintenance of the facility paved the way for the poorly lit displays, cracking walls, and dusty specimens. The mislabeled displays that conveyed incorrect scientific information, primitive drawings in lieu of stuffed or preserved specimens of common flora and fauna, and absence of whole areas of knowledge typically covered in displays of natural history came as more of a surprise.

The rooms that displayed the Lake Turkana (formerly Lake Rudolf) fossils and other materials on hominid evolution stood in sharp contrast to the rest of the museum. These rooms were well-lit and maintained, the specimens accurately labeled, and the latest theories regarding hominid evolution presented. I noticed the plaque indicating that these rooms and displays had been financed and developed by the Leakey family, with support from well-known anthropologists and paleontologists from Europe and the United States.

Even more amazing than the rooms and displays themselves, and perhaps mirroring the physical contrast, was the apparent racial/nationality separation of the people who spent time in the different rooms viewing the displays. Almost all of the people who appeared to be tourists from other countries and were White spent the bulk of their time poring over the displays of hominid evolution; they passed quickly through the other rooms, barely glancing, if they stopped at all, at the poorly lit and barely maintained displays on other topics, including those on the culture of Africa and Kenya. In contrast, the Kenyan people, including numerous groups of teachers and schoolchildren, who were Black, seemed to go through the rooms devoted to hominid evolution only out of necessity to reach additional rooms with other displays; they rarely looked at the hominid displays and any student who paused too long near such a display appeared to be hurried on by the teacher. This museum experience, with its apparent separation of cultures, made me reflect upon the continuing colonization of Kenya by the scientists and tourists from Northern continents.

Brief interactions coupled with more lengthy observations of Kenyans during the visit provided the third insight. A relatively small group of Kenyans appeared to have the scientific, educational, and technological skills normally considered necessary to compete in the increasingly technological global economy. This elite usually had been educated outside of the country, often in Britain, the colonizing country; sometimes they had been educated in one of the very good elite boarding schools in Kenya, which require high test scores and much money. Because their education focuses beyond their country, on issues defined as significant from a global perspective, Kenyans trained in these schools have access to technology, as well as the science and technology literacy skills to use the technology.

Although interested in science and technology and highly motivated toward education, the vast majority of Kenyans lack access to the proper education and the technology itself to become competitive as defined by the technological global economy. For example, the school in which my daughter taught was a Marambee tribal school, which tended to focus locally, on issues important to the country, and which is, notably, lowest on the totem pole for resources. Unless large numbers of individuals from schools like this, where the majority receive their education, acquire the access permitting them to join the elite and/or the elite shares more of its skills and resources with the majority, it appears that the country, after internal political and economic strife, will have increasing difficulty competing in the global economy. Women and girls form a particularly small proportion of the educationally and technologically elite.

Lives of Immigrant Women Scientists in Canada

During late September 1996, I had been invited to Saskatoon in Saskatchewan, Canada, to deliver the opening keynote address for a conference called "Women and Other Faces of Science." Although the conference included scholars from several countries and had an international focus, most participants came from provinces across Canada, with a sizable showing of faculty from the United States. In addition to the slightly different perspective and reflection on one's discipline and scholarship that often result from experiencing how the subject and its surrounding issues are approached in another country, two speakers in separate panel sessions jolted my thinking about postcolonialism, feminism, and science.

The first speaker, from the National Science Foundation in the United States, presented the latest statistics on women graduate students and doctorate recipients in U.S. universities. Even though I knew the speaker and had myself served as Senior Program Officer for Women's Programs at the NSF during the preceding year, one aspect of the data she presented completely surprised me. The chart dividing doctoral recipients by country of citizenship, as well as gender, revealed that an increasingly significant proportion, 39.7% in 1996, of Ph.D.s in science, engineering, and mathematics awarded to women by U.S. universities went to non-U.S. citizens—that is, women from other countries (NSF, 1997b, Table 3). Although well aware of the data concerning the increasingly large percentage of foreign-born graduate students in the United States, I labored under the impression that virtually all of these students were male. In fact, 22.2% of doctorates awarded to non-U.S. citizens go to women (NSF, 1997b, Table 3). I had attended numerous discussions surrounding the issue of foreign graduate students and the "problems" they caused for the U.S. science, engineering, and mathematics enterprise, since Congress viewed them as using resources intended for U.S. nationals, while most departments sought these bright, hardworking students to sustain their graduate enrollments, although admitting that their presence often caused some frictions.

One of the issues often raised in such discussions focused on the gender and science problems that resulted from having large numbers of foreign male graduate students in many U.S. science, engineering, and mathematics departments. Coming from cultures in which roles for women and expectations for interactions between women and men students and professionals differ considerably from such roles and expectations in the United States, foreign male graduate students have become one of the factors listed as a deterrent for women in science. Behaviors ranging from a failure to understand that repeated requests from a foreign male teaching assistant to date an undergraduate student constitute sexual harassment, to foreign male graduate students refusing to work on projects with and/or take their female peers seriously as scientists, have been suggested to be part of the chilly environment deterring women from science, engineering, and mathematics in the United States. Never in any of these discussions did the foreign female graduate student emerge. The fact of the dramatic increase in the percentages of foreign female graduate students in recent years was absent, as was any mention of what sorts of "chilly environments" these women might be experiencing as they sought Ph.D.s in SEM in the United States.

The next day in a separate panel session, an activist from the community provided some context and details that described how very chilly the environment for these women really can be. Born in Pakistan, the speaker had emigrated to Canada and now worked as a refugee/immigrant trainer in the Job Re-Entry Program to facilitate the decision of women from other countries to settle in Canada and find employment in their new home country. Women scientists and engineers, particularly those who had come to Canada with their husbands, constituted a substantial fraction of the women immigrants/refugees enrolled in the program. The following summary, handed out by the speaker and brought to life through her illustrations of case histories of three individual women, graphically depicts the plight of these women:

> There were 12 women in the Job Re-Entry Program last year. Three of them were engineers, two medical doctors, one with a master's degree in Biology, and another with a Ph.D. in Horticulture. Others were nurses, social workers and accountants. All of these women were employed in the service industry such as cleaning, dishwashing and babysitting prior to being accepted in JRE. After the six-month job training, they all lost jobs. Some have moved out of Saskatoon; others have gone back to the service industry. (Nayar, 1996, n.p.)

The speaker described the maltreatment of the immigrant scientists and engineers who were the husbands of these women, by the North American (Canadian) university, industrial, and scientific establishment. Far from being welcomed into good, high-paying jobs appropriate for their training and credentials, most fought for acceptance as students into Canadian graduate programs in fields in which they had already received a Ph.D. in their country of origin. Because their degrees came from universities in so-called "third-world" or "developing" countries, the North American scientists and engineers did not perceive them as "true" scientists with credentials acceptable to undertake serious work in North America.

The women scientists and engineers who had accompanied their husbands to Canada feared and faced even worse discrimination and devaluation of their credentials. Many placed as top priority having their husbands retrained to stabilize the future of the family income. Watching the struggles and discrimination faced by their husbands left the women scientists demoralized and extremely wary of how they would fare with the scientific establishment since they bore the burdens of being women and wives, in addition to the stigmas of race and origin from a third-world country borne by their husbands. The story of Ms. J serves as a case in point:

> Name: Ms. J
> Country of Origin: China
> Educational Background: Master in Engineering
> Occupation in China: Engineer
> Occupation in Saskatoon: (before JRE) waitress in a Chinese restaurant
> Ms. J and her husband came to Saskatoon in 1990. They are both engineers. He has gone back to school (with lots of difficulty he was admitted to the College of Engineering). She worked as a waitress to support him.
> Ms. J applied to JRE program and got in. She was able to find a job placement in SEDCO. However, after the funding for this placement was over, she became unemployed. She wants to go back to school but feels she will never get a job in engineering. (Nayar, 1996, n.p.)

This and other case histories caused me to reflect that virtually all discussions of foreign-born male scientists and their effects on "women in science," have centered on impacts on North American-born women scientists, with no discussion of this other group of women scientists—the foreign-born wives/women. The speaker proceeded to give a sophisticated analysis of why these women scientists from developing countries find little or no acceptance by the North American scientific establishment. She suggested that science in the North American culture fills the legacy of religion in some other societies. This means that only a chosen few are entitled to become scientists. Those entitled to become scientists usually include heterosexual, privileged, White men. Others who differ from these scientists because of their gender, race, class, or sexual orientation become the "other" to scientists. As racialized women from developing countries, the immigrant women become the "other of others."

I realized that the "other of others" typically have been perceived as a human laboratory upon whom drugs considered too risky for North American populations are tested; their homeland may be perceived as a colonized territory where piracy, appropriation, and exploitation of resources, herbs, treatments, and methods are permitted. Although indigenous people of the colonized world and women in developed countries have done science since antiquity (Bernal, 1987; Needham, 1969; Weatherford, 1988), their contributions to the evolution of modern science have been largely erased from history. Pharmaceutical companies, industry, and science currently exhibit considerable interest in "indigenous science," but their approach tends to emphasize "discovery and patenting" by first-world scientists of medicines and science traditional to the third world.

Sweden's Use of Education as a Colonizing Strategy

From the conference in Saskatchewan I flew directly to Stockholm and took the train to Linkoping University. Because the Swedish parliament had legislated that gender must be integrated into science and technology, I had been invited to propose a research agenda exploring feminist and women's issues in biology, biotechnology, and reproductive technology research. During the course of casual conversations, two comments urged me to think further about postcolonialism and women in science.

The first comment related to a newly initiated program in ethnic/multicultural studies, for which the same college that houses the gender studies program had just received funding. Some faculty mentioned in passing that ethnic studies and gender studies had been the only programs to receive new money. Congratulating my hosts, I asked about collaborative research initiatives that gender and ethnic studies planned to pursue together. They looked puzzled and explained that the programs were quite separate, with the exception of their common interests in science, technology, and society, which they shared with all programs in the college. The intersection of race/ethnicity with gender, perspectives of women of color, and shared concerns and theoretical bases of women's and ethnic studies seemed to be new concepts to the faculty of both programs. They explained that the influx of immigrants from other countries to the previously relatively homogeneous population of Sweden provided an impetus for ethnic/multicultural studies, although they recognized that the United States and other countries with a more heterogeneous population had pioneered these studies. These comments prodded me to recount the new insights I had just obtained regarding women scientists from developing countries who had immigrated to North America. My hosts suggested that such individuals, as well as native Laplander scientists, probably faced discrimination in Sweden, although they also had not considered the situation for immigrant women scientists.

The second insight regarding postcolonialism emerged when a faculty member responded to a question I had asked regarding Swedish universities. She explained that Sweden had often placed universities in colonies, consciously recognizing that education by the culture of the colonizing country provides a mechanism for transforming/assimilating the colony to become a more integral part of the colonizer. She emphasized that after Uppsala, established in 1477, the next Swedish universities had been Dorpat (Tartu) in Estonia in 1632, Abo in 1610, and Lund in 1668, all developed to make the new territories more Swedish. Today, only Lund remains as "Swedish" (Elisabeth Sundin, personal communication, September 1996).

The portion of this history of higher education in Sweden that I found fascinating and relevant was the notion of education as a conscious colonizing strategy. I wondered to what extent the North American attitude toward not accepting the science and credentials of scientists from developing countries constitutes a form of colonialism. When they receive the stamp of approval from North American universities or researchers after education in this system, have they become assimilated as part of the colonizing country? How does this correspond to the current debate in K–12 education in the United States over the tension between bilingual and multicultural education and the need for a common language and unified curriculum? Is the documented sexism in education, particularly in the male-dominated fields of SEM, an integral part of the colonizing function of education?

These disparate experiences in Kenya, Canada, and Sweden convinced me that postcolonial feminism might provide a unique, untapped perspective through which to explore new research agendas, education, and workforce issues surrounding women and science in the United States. Although disciplines in the humanities and social sciences have employed postcolonial critiques for fruitful explorations of literature, culture, and social interactions, only recently have the philosophers of science (Haraway, 1989, 1992, 1997; Harding, 1993, 1998) begun to apply postcolonial critiques to the natural and physical sciences. Their applications have tended to focus on theoretical and language issues, rather than on practical implications for research agendas, education, and the workforce.

IMPLICATIONS OF POSTCOLONIAL
SCIENTIFIC/TECHNOLOGICAL INTERACTIONS IN PRACTICE

Not surprisingly, scientific research agendas, the educational system, and workforce issues reflect the varying complex aspects of the interrelationship among developed and developing countries in general and between the particular cultures of the colonized and colonizing country. General themes include the underdevelopment of the third world by Europe and the West (Harding, 1993); ignoring, obscuring, or misappropriating earlier scientific achievements and history of third-world countries; the fascination with so-called "indigenous science"; and the recognition that third-world countries must become scientifically and technologically literate to join and compete in a global economy. The particular forms and ways that these general themes take shape and play out with regard to gender issues vary, depending partially on the history, culture, and geography of both the colonized and colonizing countries, and the duration of colonization.

The failure of Northern scientists and societies to understand the history of science and technology in Southern countries, coupled with past and current racism and sexism, may partially explain three of the major trends of postcolonial scientific/technological interactions discussed at length in this volume.

1. Use of developing countries in Southern continents to dump outmoded and/or unsafe technologies and drugs that no longer are considered appropriate for use in Northern/developed countries
2. Exploitation of the physical environments of Southern continents and physical bodies of people living in these countries as test sites for chemicals, drugs, and technologies deemed too risky for Northern/developed countries and populations
3. Exploration and appropriation of medicines, herbs, and indigenous science from developing/Southern countries by scientists and corporate employees from multinational corporations to "discover" their scientific potential and patent them for use in Northern science and medicine

Each trend will be discussed further below.

Because women in Southern countries tend to have less power and status than men, they bear the consequences of these interactions disproportionately. For example, many of the outmoded contraceptives ruled "unsafe" for use in the United States find their way to markets in developing countries. Pharmaceutical companies currently market intrauterine devices and high-dose progesterone pills and have marketed Norplant, as discussed in Chapter 4, and Depo-provera, in developing countries, when these contraceptives were banned from sale in the United States (Gillespie, 1998; Washburn, 1996).

When the trend against breast-feeding shifted, causing larger numbers of first-world women to nurse their babies to provide antibodies and other health benefits, Northern companies marketed formula in developing Southern countries. The formula caused complications for women and their infants that were rare or unknown in developed countries: The absence of hormone shots to dry up the milk meant women went through the painful "drying up" process without the aid of drugs. Since lactation served to suppress ovulation, particularly in regions where women experienced marginal nutrition, the use of formula shortened the interval between pregnancies. When the free formula ran out or was scarce and money was unavailable, remaining quantities of formula were stretched through dilution with water. Contaminated water gave the babies diarrhea and exposure to intestinal parasites at a much earlier age than they would have experienced had they been nursed, and without the immunity from antibodies passed through mother's milk.

Cesarean sections, although not a new technology, have risen recently in developing countries at an alarming rate. In some Latin American regions, between 30% and 80% (Barros, Vaughn, Victoria, & Huttly, 1991; Good Maust, 1996) of babies currently result from cesarean births. Women who undergo cesarean section have a 20–50% chance of developing an infection, which requires careful post partum follow-up medical attention, including the importation of medical technology to areas poorly equipped to use or maintain the equipment. Knowledge of cesareans, which involves the use of imported technology, nonlocal pharmaceuticals, and nonlocal resources, expands to the detriment of local systems of obstetrical care, developed over centuries. The system of medical care is implemented to fix emergencies rather than contribute to health using systems evolved for a particular population in a specific environment throughout centuries.

At the same time that developing Southern countries serve as markets for dumping unsafe drugs and technologies considered unsafe for Northern populations but desirable for profits, the environments and bodies, particularly those of the female population, become test sites for new drugs considered too risky for the developed world. The history of testing of high-estrogen oral contraceptives in Puerto Rican women during the 1960s serves as a historical case in point.

In Puerto Rico 132 women received high-dose estrogen oral contraceptives for 12 months before the pill was put on the market in the mainland United States. In addition to the issues surrounding racism and sexism, coupled with the risk involved, informed consent became an issue. Questions of bilingualism and literacy surfaced when some of the women upon whom the contraceptives were tested indicated their impression that the pills would enhance fertility, rather than prevent conception (Zimmerman et al., 1980).

More recently, the use of Depo-provera as a contraceptive in women in third-world countries, often supported by USAID funding, provided Upjohn Company with a market for its product when FDA approval was held up until 1992 after 18 years of being denied in the United States (Washburn, 1996). It also paved the way for usage of the drug in African Americans, Native Americans, and women of lower socioeconomic status in the United States, although some evidence suggests use in these women without proper consent before FDA approval (Washburn, 1996).

Just as women's bodies in developing countries have been exploited for testing and dumping, so have the physical environments. Since in many parts of the world women maintain the physical environment, particularly the forests, ignoring women's knowledge of the environment results in double exploitation of them. Vandana Shiva (1989) eloquently describes how the British colonizers ignored indigenous knowledge, particularly women's knowledge, of forestry and subsistence economy in their initial colonization efforts:

> When the British colonised India, they first colonised her forests. Ignorant of their wealth and of the wealth of knowledge of local people to sustainably manage the forests, they displaced local rights, local needs and local knowledge and reduced this primary source of life into a timber mine. Women's subsistence economy based on the forest was replaced by the commercial economy of British colonialism. (p. 306)

In the current postcolonial era, the West continues to ignore women's knowledge of forestry:

> Since it is women's work that protects and conserves nature's life in forestry and in agriculture, and through such conservation work, sustains human life through ensuring the provision of food and water, the destruction of the integrity of forest ecosystems is most vividly and concretely experienced by peasant women. For them forestry is married to food production; it is essential for providing stable, perennial supplies of water for drinking and for irrigation, and for providing the fertility directly as green manure or as organic matter cycled through farm animals. Women's agricultural work in regions like the Himalaya is largely work in and with the forest, yet it is discounted both in forestry and in agriculture. (p. 309)

This ignorance and misunderstanding result in "development projects" planned by Northern-dominated organizations to improve and "green" the environment in developing countries, which lead to a reduction of biodiversity, loss of food, and destruction of the water cycle:

> A case study of World Bank sponsored social forestry in Kolar district of Karnataka is an illustration of reductionism and maldevelopment in forestry being extended to farmland. Decentred agroforestry, based on multiple species and private and common treestands, has been India's age-old strategy for maintaining farm productivity in arid and semi-arid zones. The *honge*,

tamarind, jack-fruit and mango, the *jola, gobli, kagli* and bamboo traditionally provided food and fodder, fertilizer and pesticide, fuel and small timber. The backyard of each rural home was a nursery, and each peasant woman the sylviculturalist. The invisible, decentred agroforestry model was significant because the humblest of species and the smallest of people could participate in it, and with space for the small, *everyone* was involved in protecting and planting.

The reductionist mind took over tree planting with "social forestry." Plans were made in national and international capitals by people who could not know the purpose of the *honge* and the *neem*, and saw them as weeds. The experts decided that indigenous knowledge was worthless and "unscientific," and proceeded to destroy the diversity of indigenous species by replacing them with row after row of eucalyptus seedlings in polythene bags, in government nurseries. . . .

In the context of ecological cycles and of the food needs of people and livestock, the eucalyptus actually makes negative contributions. It is destructive to nature's work and women's work in agriculture, for by destroying the water and land and organic matter base for food production, women's productivity in sustenance is killed. Lolar, which is the most successful social forestry district in Karnataka, has already lost more than 13 percent of its agricultural land to eucalyptus cultivation; most of this has been at the cost of its staple food, the millet, *ragi*, and associated food crops. (Shiva, 1989, pp. 311–312)

In a similar fashion, clear cutting of forests and placement of dams in rivers initiated by Western/Northern scientists and engineers in Thailand have led to drastic changes in the weather, environment, and ultimately the health of the people:

There is, for example, the cultural fragmentation that occurs after the forests' destruction: of communities that once depended for food, clothing, medicine, shelter, and tools, as well as spiritual sustenance, on intact ecosystems. The increasing centralization of the state, and the intensification of resource use of industrial development, is causing the gradual erosion not only of natural resources but also of people's customary rights to land, cultural integrity, local knowledge and sense of belonging. For people living in a weakened environment, the goods and services that were derived to a significant extent from nature must now, increasingly, be replaced by the market. But purchasing food or drug or cultural commodities (through television, for example) demands the exchange of items that have the equivalent outside market value, forcing people either to extract more and more from the ecosystem, or to leave the village altogether. In the extreme case, when nature is so degraded that it can no longer provide, one of the only remaining local resources in the community that has value on the market is the bodies of the young. In those places where adolescent women—and, to a lesser extent, men—leave home to sell their labor in the sex industry, AIDS, which appears to have infected a huge proportion of the country's half-million prostitutes, has become a physical manifestation of political dispossession. (Usher, 1994, p. 11)

The "dumping" and "testing" mentality indicates the disregard with which Northern scientists and corporations hold the scientific achievements, culture, and people, especially the women, who live in Southern developing countries. An ironic twist in the postcolonial interactions is that Northern countries simultaneously demonstrate a fascination with herbs, plants, and healing techniques, including those developed and known by women, traditionally used in these cultures. This ironic twist is exemplified by the United States seeking a patent, protested by public demonstrations in India, on the antifungal and insect-killing components of the neem tree, formerly deemed a "weed" and replaced by eucalyptus plantings in earlier U.S.-sponsored "development" projects (King & Stabinsky, 1999). Pharmaceutical companies and other corporations based in Northern countries currently invest considerable resources in attempting to learn "natural" cures known by indigenous people, particularly medicine men, midwives, and women healers. These attempts range from relatively high tech extractions of the medicinally active ingredients from plants and herbs (Mooney, 1998) to California companies such as Shaman Pharmaceuticals paying sociolinguists and other anthropologists to describe and translate the meanings of words, thereby identifying plants likely to hold medicinal properties.

Bioprospecting for indigenous knowledge of plants and seeds by the pharmaceutical and biotechnology industries typically has resulted in a transfer of knowledge from the indigenous community to the corporation, where the information becomes protected as intellectual property rights through a contract. Even in the much-publicized cases of Shaman (Shiva, 1997) and Merck (Blum, 1993; Carr, Pedersen, & Ramaswamy, 1993), where the industry has attempted to compensate the developing countries for their contributions, the amount of compensation remains minuscule relative to the profits for the industry. Furthermore, the agreements tend to be with neither the indigenous people nor their government, but with conservation groups.

Thus, in 1991 Merck paid $1 million for the right to keep and analyze plant samples gathered from national Costa Rican rain forest parks. In contrast, the revenues of Merck are $4 billion a year, and a conservation group (neither the people living near the park nor the government) negotiated the agreement. Similarly, in 1992 Eli Lilly paid Shaman Pharmaceuticals $4 million for exclusive marketing rights to antifungal drugs developed from the information provided by native healers. Shaman's nonprofit arm, the Healing Forest Conservancy, has agreed to return an undisclosed amount to the countries in which the bioprospecting company works (Shiva, 1997).

The contracts and intellectual property rights agreements lead to eventual obscuring of indigenous rights and knowledge. Shiva (1997) states the case most eloquently:

> The concept of adding value through bioprospecting hides the removal and destruction of the value of indigenous plants and knowledge. As the genes of a particular plant gain value, the plant itself becomes dispensable, especially if the genes can be replicated in vitro. As useful characteristics of plants are identified by indigenous communities, the communities themselves—along with their lifestyles and knowledge systems—become dispensable. (p. 74)

A reflection of Northern scientists' continuing arrogance and ignorance, simultaneous with their fascination with indigenous science, is the patenting by first-world scientists of the "discovery" of the herbs or active chemicals from these herbs and plants used for hundreds and even thousands of years by the indigenous peoples. A woman from Pakistan told me that she feared that the price of turmeric, which she enjoyed using in her curries, would rise astronomically (Javed Nayar, personal communication, September 1996). She explained that Western scientists had just "discovered" that the spice might be useful against cancer because it had been used by the indigenous people to cure the disease for decades. She worries that pharmaceutical companies will patent turmeric, thereby causing the price to rise.

These postcolonial interactions surrounding research, testing, and policy reveal a combination of ignorance and fascination with science and medicine in Southern continents. The Northern universities that educate and the industries that employ scientists, engineers, mathematicians, and physicians replicate these neocolonial approaches toward people from Southern countries. In short, some of these postcolonial interactions in research and development become translated into workforce/education interactions in the United States.

EDUCATION AND WORKFORCE INTERACTIONS

Statistics collected by the U.S. federal government reveal an increasing proportion of foreign-born graduate students pursuing science, engineering, and mathematics graduate degrees in recent years. Foreign students accounted for the large growth in master's and doctoral degrees in science and engineering fields over the past 15 years, with nearly half of the approximately 400,000 foreign students enrolled in 1991–92 studying science and engineering (NSB, 1996). Although foreign students obtain only a small fraction of undergraduate degrees, they obtain 25% of master's degrees and 47% of doctorates in science and engineering (NSF, 1996). Between 1977 and 1993, the number of U.S. science and engineering master's degrees obtained by foreign students more than doubled; during the same period, the number of foreign students receiving doctoral degrees tripled. In contrast, the number of U.S. citizens receiving master's and doctoral degrees during this period in these fields remained relatively stable (NSF, 1996).

Although the numbers of foreign-born individuals in the science, engineering, and mathematics civilian labor force also have increased, the percentage remains much lower than that of students. For example, in 1993, 23% of science and engineering doctorate holders residing in the United States were foreign born (NSF, 1996). The variations of foreign born among the disciplines ranged from 40.3% in engineering to 13.1% in the social sciences (NSF, 1996). Because of the Immigration Act of 1990, which permitted large increases in employment-based quotas for highly skilled workers, 1992 marked a large increase of 62% in admissions of scientists and engineers over the 1991 immigration levels; 1993 saw continued increases. The proportion of female scientists and engineers immigrating to the United States has increased consistently over time, with women representing 21.3% of scientists and engineers admitted with permanent resident status in 1993 (NSB, 1996). In 1998, controversy arose over loss of jobs to Americans when the 65,000 cap for visas for foreigners to work in industry was reached in May and the Senate voted to raise the cap (Lederman, 1998).

The combination of increasing numbers of foreign-born graduate students and shrinking resources has led Congress to consider restricting legislation regarding federal support for foreign-born students and faculty. Universities have provided mixed responses to this trend. Many science, engineering, and mathematics departments have fought the restrictions (Lederman, 1998), particularly those targeted toward graduate and postdoctoral students, because of their desire to continue to have large numbers of highly qualified students to support their research at a time when the numbers of qualified U.S.-born science, engineering, and mathematics students are shrinking. Faculty and administrators often have supported restrictions on employment of foreign-born citizens, hoping to preserve higher salaries and limit the numbers of qualified applicants to the profession. However, some wished to hire the outstanding

foreign-born scientists at cheaper salaries than their American counterparts (Lederman, 1998).

A considerable literature, as discussed earlier in this chapter, has
evolved surrounding the issue of the problems of foreign-born males
creating a "chilly climate" for women in science (Brush, 1991; Hall &
Sandler, 1982). The authors of a published survey of employment opportunities advised women to avoid businesses and departments where the
men in power were foreign born (Fader, 1990). Research in sociolinguistics
and cross-cultural communication (Gumperz, 1982; Tannen, 1990; Wolfson, 1989) has established that people of different language and cultural
backgrounds often have divergent interpretations of the same verbal and
nonverbal behavior. This research has been interpreted as suggesting that,
in addition to gender differences, cross-cultural communication difficulties and value differences held by their U.S. male counterparts, contribute
to foreign-born males' having a negative impact on the retention of women
in science, engineering, and mathematics.

Racist and neocolonial attitudes may infuse these discussions and
interpretations of the role foreign-born men play in deterring women
from science. The lack of mention of the increasing numbers of foreign-
born women graduate students in science and scientists attempting to
enter the workforce, may reveal a lack of awareness or of sensitivity to
these foreign-born women on the part of U.S.-born women in science.

In a survey that asked women scientists and engineers to name the
most significant issues/challenges/opportunities facing women scientists
today as they plan their careers (Rosser & Zieseniss, 1999), a 1997 recipient
of the POWRE award, given by the prestigious National Science Foundation, wrote the following:

> When competing for an entry-level job as the only woman against two
> Russian emigres in their late forties for a department with a poor record of
> retaining women, I was told that age-discrimination laws applied. Selective
> decision-making by the EOAA office left me at a disadvantage rather than
> an advantage. For another position, the department head told me I had no
> bargaining position because I was applying for an affirmative action slot. I
> have seen very progressive policies enunciated at the provost's level, only
> to see that their execution is left to the discretion and values of a department
> head. (Respondent 17)

Although some indicators suggest that more money is going into
scientific research, especially in medicine and computer and information
sciences, resources remain tight. In such times, which spawn fewer jobs
and severe competition for grants, women scientists must strive to understand the situation and include the issues of foreign-born women scien-

tists, particularly those from Southern countries, in the struggles of women scientists. U.S.-born women scientists must be especially wary, in this era of attacks on affirmative action and backlash, not to let our minor successes in the scientific establishment separate us from the struggle of women scientists from Southern, developing countries.

Recognition that the treatment and placement of foreign-born women scientists are very close to the position of most U.S.-born women scientists within the scientific hierarchy, leads to an understanding of the need to improve the situation for all women scientists. Educating ourselves and teaching our students about the contributions of the Southern continents to the history of science and technology, exploring the current, specific interactions between scientists in our subdiscipline and scientists in Southern countries, and finding out the numbers of women scientists from developing countries in our local community serve as initial, personal steps in the process of understanding the situation of this unrecognized group of women scientists. Such steps taken by individual women may lead to pathways to develop more comprehensive models that will include all women in the global science and technology enterprise.

Why This Union Will Save Science, the Lives of Other Women, and Ourselves

FORMING COALITIONS BETWEEN women scientists and physicians and women's studies scholars in Northern and Southern continents becomes critical for preserving indigenous women's knowledge, rights, and communities for the reasons outlined in Chapters 3, 4, and 5. These coalitions also may provide the lifeline that women scientists, physicians, and women's studies scholars—both those from Northern and those from Southern, formerly colonized countries who have experienced postcolonialism and now live in the North—need for their own professional and personal survival. I have come to believe this from observing my female colleagues and from my personal experience. Without coalitions and interdisciplinary interactions with women colleagues, isolation may lead to alienation and self-destruction, even for dedicated scientists who are knowledgeable feminists. As a woman, a feminist, and a scientist, my interdisciplinary coalitions with colleagues in women's studies, humanities, social sciences, science, and health have been critical for my 25 years of research on women/gender issues in science and health and for my professional and personal survival.

The following article, submitted by a woman colleague, Banu Subramanian, to a special issue on women and science that I was editing for a women's studies journal, underlined the critical necessity for coalitions among women in this postcolonial scientific environment.

SNOW BROWN AND THE SEVEN DETERGENTS: A META-NARRATIVE ON SCIENCE AND THE SCIENTIFIC METHOD

Once upon a time, deep within a city in the Orient, lived a young girl called Snehalatha Bhrijbhushan. She spent her childhood merrily playing in the streets with her friends while the city looked on indulgently. "That girl,

Sneha (as they called her) is going to become someone famous, someday," they would all say. Sneha soon became fascinated with the world of science. One day, she announced, "I am going to sail across the blue oceans to become a scientist!"

There was silence in the room. "But you can be a scientist here, you know?"

"Yes," said Sneha. "But I want to explore the world. There is so much out there to see and learn. I want to visit all these places."

"Where is this place?" they asked.

"It's called the land of the Blue Devils."

"But, this is dangerous country," they cried. "No one has ever been there, who has come back alive."

"Yes, I know," said Sneha. "But I have been reading about it. It is in the land of the kind and gentle people. In any case I can handle it."

Her friends and family watched her animated face and knew that if anyone could do it, it would be brave Sneha and they relented. The city watched her set out and wished her a tearful farewell. She promised to return soon and bring back tales from lands afar. For forty-two days and nights, Sneha sailed the oceans. Her face was aglow with excitement and her eyes filled with the stars. "It's going to be wonderful," she told herself.

And so, on one fine day, she arrived in the land of the Blue Devils. She went in search of the Building of Scientific Truth. When she saw it, she held her breath. There it stood tall and slender, almost touching the skies. Sneha shivered, "Don't be silly," she told herself. She entered the building. The floors were polished and gleaming white. It all looked so grand and yet so formidable. She was led into the office of the Supreme White Patriarch. The room was full. "Welcome budding Patriarchs," he said. "We at the Department of the Pursuit of Scientific Truth welcome you. But let me be perfectly frank. These are going to be difficult years ahead. This is no place for the weak or the emotional or the fickle. You have to put in long, hard hours. If you think you cannot cut it, you should leave now. Let me now introduce you to our evaluation system. Come with me."

He led them across the hall into a huge room. At the end of the room stood a mirror, long and erect and oh! So white. "This is the Room of Judgment," he continued. "The mirror will tell you how you're doing. Let me show you." He went to the mirror and said,

"Mirror, Mirror on the wall
Who is the fairest scientist of them all?"

"You are! O Supreme White Patriarch!" said the mirror. The Patriarch laughed. "That is what all of you should aspire to. And one day when it calls out your name, you will take my place. But until then, you will all seek Truth and aspire to be the number one. We want fighters here, Patriarchs with initiative and genius. And those who rank consistently the last for six months, we believe they just do not have the ability to pursue Scientific Truth and they will be expelled. Go forth, all ye budding Patriarchs and find Scientific Truth."

Everyone went their way. Sneha found herself in the middle of the hallway all alone. "Go find Truth?" she said to herself. Was this a treasure hunt? Did Truth fall off the sky? She was very confused. This is not what she thought it would be like. She went looking for her older colleagues, one of the Young Patriarchs. "Where does one find Scientific Truth?" she asked.

"Well!" said he, "First you have to find the patronage of an associate patriarch or an assistant patriarch. You will have a year to do that. Until then, you take courses they teach you and you learn about Truths already known and how to find new Truths. During this time you have to learn how to be a scientist. That is very important and the mirror will assist you in this endeavor."

"How does the mirror work?" asked Sneha.

"Well, the mirror is the collective consciousness of all the Supreme White Patriarchs across the land of the kind and gentle people. They have decided what it takes to be the ideal scientist and it is what we all must dream of and aspire and work toward if we want to find Scientific Truth. You must check with the mirror as often as you can to monitor your progress." Sneha tiptoed to the Room of Judgment and stood in front of the mirror and said,

"Mirror, mirror on the wall
Who is the fairest scientist of them all?"

The mirror replied,

"Not you, you're losing this game
You with the unpronounceable name!"

Sneha was very depressed. Things were not going as she had expected. "Oh mirror," she cried, "Everything has gone wrong. What do I do?"

"First and foremost," said the mirror, "check Murphy's laws. They will hold you in good stead as a graduate student. Anything that can go wrong will go wrong, or haven't you heard. And if you think this is as bad as it gets, wait a few years. And stop looking so pathetic. You have to develop a sense of humor about these things!"

Sneha was now really upset. "I've just sailed forty-two days and nights leaving all my family and friends behind and am now told that I am worthless by a mirror and I should think it is funny?"

"Oh, stop being so damned emotional," said the mirror. "Stop whining. To be frank, I don't think you are cut out to be a scientist unless you're willing to really work at it."

"I've dreamed about this all my life. What should I do?"

"Well," said the mirror. "More than anything, you have to learn to act like a scientist. That's your first task. Deep within the forests around lives the Wise Matriarch in the House of the Seven Detergents. Go see her, she will help you."

Sneha set out to meet the Wise Matriarch. "Come in, child," she said. "What seems to be the problem?" She seemed a very kind woman and Sneha poured out her misery.

"I know this is a very difficult time for you but it is also a very important one," the Matriarch said.

"Why do they call you the 'Wise' Matriarch?" Sneha enquired.

"I joined the Department of the Pursuit of Scientific Truth some twenty years ago," the Matriarch replied. "That is why I understand what you're going through. I was expelled. When the Department offered me this position, I felt I could begin changing things. Over the years, I have advised many budding Patriarchs. You could say I've earned my reputation.

"My child," she said. "This is where the Department sends its scientific misfits. Let me show you what they would like me to have you do." She led Sneha to a room and in it stood seven jars. "These are the seven detergents," she said. "With them you can wash away any part of yourself you don't want. But the catch is that once you wash it away, you have lost it forever."

Sneha was excited. "Well! Firstly, I'd like to get rid of my name and my accent. The mirror told me that."

The Wise Matriarch shook her head, "My child, do not give away your identity, your culture—they are part of you, who you are," she cried.

"But," said Sneha. "I've always dreamed of being a scientist. I spent all my savings coming here. I cannot go back a failure. I understand your concern because I've noticed that the mirror did not say that to everyone. There were those from other parts of the white continents from places they called Europe that had difficult names and different accents but the mirror had no problem and was almost indulgent at times. I am treated differently. I understand that. But this is truly what I want." Sneha got into the Great Washing Machine with the first detergent. Rub-a-dub-a-dub. Rub-a-dub-a-dub, went the detergent.

"You may come out now Snow Brown, good luck."

Snow Brown went back amazed at how differently her tongue moved. For the next week she met the other budding Patriarchs and decided her course listings and went out socializing with her colleagues. But everything was new in this land. How people ate, drank. What people ate and drank. She felt stupid and ignorant. And just as she expected, when she went to the mirror, it told her that such behavior was quite unscientific and that she had to learn the right etiquette. Off she went again to the House of the Seven Detergents and used two other detergents that worked their miracles in the grand washing machine.

"Now I sound and act like everyone else," she said satisfied.

Snow Brown went to her classes. She thought them quite interesting. But the professors never looked her in the eye, they never asked her for opinions. "Maybe they think I'm stupid," she thought. In class discussions everyone said things. Some of the things they said were pretty stupid, she thought. And so, she would gather up her courage and contribute only to be met with stony silence. On some occasions others would make the same point and the professor would acknowledge it and build on it.

She knew the mirror would be unhappy with her and sure enough she was right. "You have to be more aggressive," it said. "It doesn't matter as much what you say as how much you say."

"But that's ridiculous," she said. "Most of what is said is just plain stupid. Have you listened to some of them? They like the sound of their voices so much."

"That may be true, but that is the way. You have to make an impression and sitting and listening like a lump of clay is not the way. And another thing, why did you let the others operate the machine in lab? You have to take initiative."

"That was a $10,000 machine. What if I broke it? I've never used it before."

"Leave your Third World mentalities behind. The Patriarchs see it as a lack of initiative. They think you are not interested. You have to shoot for number one, be the very best. You have to act like a scientist, like a winner. Girl, what you need it a good dose of arrogance and some ego."

Snow Brown was a little perturbed. She was disturbed by what she saw around her. Did she really want to act like some of the people she had met? What happened to kindness, a little humility, helping each other? Just how badly did she want this, anyway? Her family was going to hate her when she went back. They would not recognize her. She thought long and hard and finally decided to go ahead with it.

She went back to the House of the Seven Detergents and used the anti-third world detergent and when she emerged, she came striding out, pride oozing out of every pore. The next day, the Supreme White Patriarch called for her. "So what kind of progress are you making in your search for Scientific Truth?" he asked.

"Well," she said. "The mirror has kept me occupied with learning to act like a scientist. Surely you can't expect me to make as much progress as the others all considering."

"We don't like students making excuses, Snow Brown. You had better make some progress and real soon. There is no place for laziness here."

Snow Brown started developing some of her ideas. So, she went to the Great Mirror to talk them over.

"I'm thinking of working with mutualisms," she said. "Organisms associate with each other in numerous ways ecologically. They can both compete for the same resources as in competition. Some live off other organisms and that's called parasitism. When organisms get into ecological relationships with each other that are mutually beneficial, it's called a mutualism."

"Well, to be frank, Snow Brown, I would recommend studying competition or parasitism."

"But most of the studies of ecological interactions have focused on them," Snow Brown said. "I am amazed that there has been so little study of mutualisms. We know of some examples. But just how prevalent they are is still up in the air. For all you know, they may be a fundamental principle that describes demographic patterns of organisms on our planet."

"Whoa! Whoa!" cried the mirror. "You're getting carried away with your emotions. We would all like a 'and they lived happily ever after' kind of fairy tale. You are violating one of the fundamentals of doing science—'objectivity.' You don't pursue a study because you 'think it would be nice.' You base it on concrete facts, data. Then you apply the Scientific Method and investigate the problem."

"I do agree that the Scientific Method may have merit," she said. "I will use it to study mutualisms too. But, tell me, why do you think competition has been so well studied?"

"That's because they are so important. Just look around you," the mirror replied. "Are the Patriarchs working with each other for their mutual benefit or are they competing? This is what I do—promote competition. It is nature's way."

"Aha!" cried Snow Brown triumphantly. "You throw emotionalism and subjectivity at me. Listen to yourself. You are reading into nature what you see in yourself. I happen to believe that mutualisms are very important in the world. The Patriarchs have decided to work with a particular model. It doesn't mean that it's the only way. It is not for example the way of some of my people. There are some studies to back me up."

"But many more to back me up and you are not with your people, little one," said the mirror laughing. "Besides, get realistic. You need the patronage of an associate or assistant patriarch. You need to get money from the Supreme White Patriarch to do the research. That's a lot of people to convince on a whim of an idea, don't you think? Don't forget you need to please the Patriarch to get ahead. I am the collective consciousness, remember? And you are still way behind in the game. This is not the time or you the person to get radical."

Convinced that pragmatism was the best course, the supremely overconfident Snow Brown developed her ideas, talked in classes, aggressively engaged the Patriarchs in dialogues. She was supremely happy. Things were finally going her way. She went to the mirror and said,

"Mirror, mirror on the wall
Who is the fairest scientist of them all?"
And the mirror replied,
"It sure ain't you Snow Brown
You're still the last one in town."
Snow Brown could not believe her ears. "I act and think like everyone around me. I am even obnoxious at times. What could I be possibly doing wrong this time?"

"Well," said the mirror. "You are overdoing it. You don't know everything. You should be a little more humble and subservient."

"Am I hearing things? I don't see anyone else doing that. This place does not validate that. You told me that yourself. What is really going on here?"

"When I advised you last," answered the mirror, "I advised you like I would advise anyone but I've been watching how the other Patriarchs interact with you. Apparently their expectations of you are different. You're brown, remember?"

Snow Brown was furious. She stormed out and went to the house of detergents and the sixth detergent washed her brownness away. She was now Snow White. She marched back to the Department of Scientific Truth. All the Patriarchs stared at her. They suddenly realized that what stood before them was a woman, and a beautiful woman at that.

"Well, am I white enough for the lot of you now?" she demanded.

"Oh! But you're too pretty to be a scientist," cried the Supreme Patriarch.

"But you can be a technician in my lab," cried another. "No! In mine," cried yet another.

The Wise Matriarch had been right. She had now lost her whole identity and for what? Why did she not see this coming, she asked herself. How could she ever have been the "fairest" scientist? How could she have been anything but last when judged by a mirror that wanted to produce clones of the Supreme White Patriarchs? She went to the House of the Seven Detergents.

"It's too late, my child," said the Wise Matriarch. "You cannot go back now. I warned you about it. I wish I had more resources to support you and others like you. I have seen this happen far too often. It is important for you to communicate this to others. You must write down what has happened to you for future generations."

Two days later, they discovered her cold body on the floor of her room. Her face looked tortured—her eyes sunken and in them lay a resigned look of someone who had nothing more to lose to the world she had come to live in. On the night stand by her body, rested the tale of "Snow Brown and the Seven Detergents."

End 1: And Injustice Prevails . . .

The Patriarchs stood around the body. "It is so sad," they said. "But she was too emotional, a very fuzzy thinker. Some people are just not meant to pursue Scientific Truth. I wish they would learn, accept it and leave instead of creating all this melodrama." The other Patriarchs nodded in agreement at the unfortunate event. "There is no reason for anyone to see this story, is there?" The Others concurred. They poured the last detergent on her. There was nothing left. No pathetic face, no ugly reminders, no evidence.

End 2: Into Empiricism . . .

Snow Brown in her subversive wisdom sent copies of her story and insights to all in the department. There were some who kept it alive. It soon became apparent that there were dissenters within the Patriarchy. They broke their silence and the movement slowly grew. Scientists began forming coalitions, talking and supporting each other in forming pockets of resistance. They questioned the power inequities. Why are most Patriarchs white? Why are most men? Over many decades, the negotiations continued. Women scientists and scientists of color rose up in the power structure. The collective consciousness was now male, female, and multicolored. But it was still supreme. It was privileged. The Pursuit for Truth continued although new truths emerged—truths from the perspective of women, from the black, brown, yellow, red and the white. The world had become a better place.

End 3: A Postmodern Fantasy . . .

The story of Snow Brown spread like wild fire. The land of the Blue Devils was ablaze with anger and rage. The Wise Matriarch and a number of budding Patriarchs stormed the Department of the Pursuit of Scientific Truth and took it over. The Great Mirror was brought down. The Room of Judgment was transformed into the Room of Negotiation. In their first historical meeting all the scientists sat together. "We need a different model," they said. They dismantled the position of the Supreme White Patriarch, the Emeritus Patriarch, the Associate Patriarch, the Assistant Patriarch and the Young Patriarch. We will be self-governing, they decided. They debunked the myth that truth was monolithic. "Truth is a myth," they said. One person's truth is often privileged over someone else's. This is dangerous. The White Patriarchs privileged their world view over all others. This distorts knowledge and an accurate description of the world. Together they decided they could help each other in reconstructing science and rewriting scientific knowledge. They ushered in the age called "the age of celebrating difference." The house of detergents was dismantled and the detergents were rendered invisible. The new Department of Scientific Endeavor was very productive. They solved many problems that had eluded the world for years. They became world renowned and their model was adopted far and wide. If you are ever in the forests in the land of the Blue Devils and come across the voice of an old school scientist arguing vociferously, you know you have stumbled across Snow Brown and the Seven Detergents. (Subramanian, in press)

PERSONAL REFLECTIONS ON MY ROLE AS A WISE MATRIARCH: THE SIGNIFICANCE OF INTERDISCIPLINARY COALITIONS

After 2 years of learning a new area of biology, my postdoctoral research finally appeared to be on track. When I became pregnant with my second child, the professor supervising my research suggested that I get an abortion, since it was "the wrong time in the research and we needed to obtain more data now to have the grant renewed." I did not have the abortion; I rationalized that taking minimal time off for childbirth meant that everything would be fine in the lab and with my scientific career. One day when I was out at noon to breast-feed the baby, a call came that focused on my area of research. Although many of the other postdocs and graduate students (all males) used their lunch hour to play squash, I later learned that the professor had made comments to others in the lab about my being off nursing again. Those comments, coupled with related incidents, made me decide to accept the offer of the new women's studies program to teach a course on biology of women.

Women's studies gave me new space, perceptions, knowledge, and connections to understand my bodily identity and the reactions it invoked. In the mid-1970s, only women were involved in this first year of the program; they welcomed me because I was a woman and even encouraged me to bring the baby to some meetings. From the stories of the more senior women in the academy, I learned that much of the discrimination I had experienced was not unique, but resulted from being a woman in a patriarchal university, which only the previous year, under court order, had dropped its official quotas on women medical students and nepotism rules against women faculty. From teaching biology of women, I began to read the evolving critiques revealing bias in research developed by men, using only males as subjects, and with theories and conclusions extrapolated inappropriately to the entire population of both men and women. While developing a new course in women's health, I recognized that despite my Ph.D. in zoology and having given birth to two children, I knew almost nothing about my own body and its functioning. When I sought materials to fill this knowledge gap, I learned that very little research had focused on women and their bodies in health and disease. Recognizing this dearth and that any research that existed had been undertaken by men from their perspective, I began to work to create materials that reflected women's experience of their biology and bodily identity. Suddenly, I felt a connection with teaching this research and with my search for materials, from medical textbooks through scientific journals to fiction, to convey the information to students. Trained in the humanities, social sciences, and fine arts, my colleagues in women's studies helped me to uncover the interdisciplinary resources needed to understand the components of women's health.

Integrating biology and women's studies into my teaching, using interdisciplinary methods and materials, seemed exciting and natural to me. This evolution of new curricular content and new teaching methods interwove the threads from my undergraduate humanities background with my years of training in the sciences. I saw inclusion of material about women in science courses as a way to attract women to the sciences.

Changing the science curriculum to include women constituted a difficult task. Seen as an innovator in this area, I became involved in a number of curriculum transformation projects at institutions throughout the nation working to integrate women's studies into traditional disciplines. In contrast, it took several years for me to realize the more positive side coming from the different bodily identity in my own research. My male colleagues had ignored me partially because of my female body, my different experiences, and my interdisciplinary interests, and because I considered alternative approaches and asked different questions from them. Eventually I recognized that their male bodies and masculine identities had limited them to partial understanding of the world they studied.

Gender bias had infected a science developed almost exclusively by men, whose bodily experiences provided them with a masculine perspective on the physical, natural world. They had given only partial, cursory examination to females of other species and had looked at the human female body from the perspective of how it suited their needs and interests.

These insights into the limitations and biases introduced by male bodies and masculine identities as a result of having virtually no women scientists, proved significant for me. I began to feel whole as I understood that my female body and the perspectives gleaned from experiences as a woman provided new venues into questions asked, research design, and theories and conclusions drawn from data in both science and health (Rosser, 1986, 1992). Scientific colleagues grudgingly admitted that perhaps feminist perspectives could be useful in science, at least in revealing gender bias. Concerns over shortages of scientists and lack of diversity in the pool of scientists sparked interest in the potential of feminist pedagogical methods and theories of women's studies to attract men of color and women to science. Both science faculty and administrators responded well to pedagogical techniques and models for integrating race and gender into the science curriculum, which I presented in *Female Friendly Science* (Rosser, 1990).

Women's studies colleagues, in addition to having substantial interest in women's health because of their own bodily experiences with the health care system, recognized the necessity to include science and health in this interdisciplinary field. Realization of the potential for obtaining grants and for interacting with faculty from the sciences, engineering, and medicine also piqued the interest of women's studies faculty in affiliating with feminist scientists. Pioneering uncharted territory, creating new vocabularies to bridge disciplines, and applying methodologies from one field to explore questions in another, helped me to fuse my bodily identity with research and academia. I envisioned an integrated identity symbolized by a positive, upward spiral, where work on feminist critiques of science, curricular transformation, pedagogy, and women's health, nourished by theoretical changes and methodological applications from the humanities and social sciences, would fuel new ideas. Colleagues from humanities, social sciences, and sciences, recognizing the benefits for science, health, and women's studies, might eagerly pursue these ideas and other interdisciplinary projects.

The vision of integration faded rapidly, as colleagues revealed their willingness to include only part of the identity. Colleagues from humanities and social sciences in women's studies often exhibited constraints and limits to accepting my academic identities. Very familiar with critiques of objectivity and the advantages of trying a variety of theoretical positions, these colleagues dismiss scientists as naive and inflexible; they cannot imagine that scientists really believe in logical positivism and objectivity. Simultaneously, because they know very little science, they fail to understand the true strengths of the scientific method, including verifiability and reliability, and that much of science really "works." Because of demonstrated gender bias, poor research design, and extrapolating beyond limits warranted by the data in some studies, they dismiss all studies as invalid or flawed. Although they live with many of the practical benefits of science and technology, their relatively low level of scientific knowledge makes them vulnerable to throwing out the baby with the bath water at the first encounter with feminist critiques of science.

Simultaneously, my scientific colleagues exhibit different, but equally constraining, limits. Although initially many scientists found feminism too radical and women's studies just a passing fad, most eventually agreed that feminists had pointed out sources of gender bias, which, when corrected, led to better science. Most scientists found feminists and their insights acceptable, as long as they remained within the liberal-feminist theoretical perspective. Since liberal feminism does not question the integrity of the scientific method itself or of its supporting corollaries of objectivity and value neutrality, my work and identity as a feminist remained acceptable to most of my scientific colleagues, as long as I stayed within a liberal-feminist theoretical framework.

I found that most scientific colleagues could accept my feminist ideas and my identity as a feminist until they learned that I thought most feminist theories, including radical, postmodern, and postcolonial feminism, provided interesting insights for science and scientists (Rosser, 1997b, 1998). Many colleagues yield the point made by socialist feminists that scientific knowledge revealed through funded research under capitalism reflects the interests of the dominant class, yet few question the notion of objectivity that such a social constructivist stance implies. Some colleagues agree that male domination of the sciences has led to exclusion of women and androcentric bias in research, while almost none support women-only research institutes as a mechanism that might be envisioned under radical feminism as a way to generate innovative ideas in a patriarchal society. Frequently colleagues involved with international projects puzzle over the ways that different developing countries have accepted/ rejected/adapted new technologies; few consider postcolonial feminist critiques to analyze the impact of the technologies on the population of those countries. I risk losing credibility when I misjudge a colleague's willingness to understand more aspects of my feminist identity and suggest an insight gleaned from postmodern or postcolonial feminism that might be useful in solving a problem.

Reading Banu's "Meta-narrative on Science and the Scientific Method" led me to question my own role as a Wise Matriarch. Although I have definitely fought to prevent *End 1: And Injustice Prevails*, I wonder whether I have placed too much faith in *End 2: Into Empiricism*. In trying to make the world "a better place" and work within the system, have I argued too strongly for coalitions, without questioning their limitations? Although *End 3: A Postmodern Fantasy* attracts me in some ways, I do still believe in science, as defined by Harding's (1991) strong objectivity; I also have some faith in the "collective consciousness" achieved through coalitions.

As women scientists and physicians who are researchers, clinicians, and educators unite to examine the impact of biotechnologies and reproductive technologies on the lives of women and society as a whole, we need to remain alert to doubts that nag us and the voices of nonscientists who warn us of potential dangers of these technologies for our own and other women's bodies and lives. Knowledge of feminist critiques of science and our own experiences as women scientists and physicians who have struggled to overcome isolation and to make our research agendas count in the scientific world, places us in a powerful and unique position to attempt to ensure that these technologies help, rather than harm, society in general and women in particular. However, that same training and experience as women scientists may make us vulnerable to overlooking the way in which these technologies may poison the environment and our own bodies. We depend on the insights and collaborations with our women's studies colleagues in humanities and social sciences, as well as the voices of women from Southern continents, to help us overcome these vulnerabilities. Our futures and fates are intertwined.

References

Achebe, Chinua. (1988). Colonialist criticism. In Achebe, *Hopes and impediments: Selected essays 1965–1987*. London: Heinemann.

Agrawal, Arun. (1995). Dismantling the divide between indigenous and scientific knowledge. *Development and Change, 26*, 413–439.

Alexander, M. Jacqui, & Chandra T. Mohanty. (Eds.). (1997). *Feminist genealogies, colonial legacies, democratic futures*. New York: Routledge.

Altbach, Phillip G. (1971). Education and neocolonialism. *Teachers College Record, 72*(1), 543–558.

Altekruse, Joan, & Sue V. Rosser. (1992). Feminism and medicine: Co-optation or cooperation? In Cheris Kramarae & Dale Spender (Eds.), *The knowledge explosion* (pp. 27–40). New York: Teachers College Press.

Altman, Roberta. (1996). *Waking up/fighting back: The politics of breast cancer*. Boston: Little, Brown.

Ambrose, Susan, Kristin Dunkle, Barbara Lazarus, Indira Nair, & Deborah Harkus. (Eds.). (1997). *Journeys of women in science and engineering: No universal constants*. Philadelphia: Temple University Press.

Antrobus, Peggy. (1995, January 17). *Visions for a new women's development agenda for the twenty-first century*. Paper delivered at PrepCom III for the World Summit on Social Development, New York.

Armstrong, B., & R. Doll. (1975). Environmental factors and cancer incidence and mortality in different countries, with special reference to dietary practice. *International Journal of Cancer, 15*, 617–631.

Arnup, Katherine, Andre Levesque, & Ruth Pierson. (1990). *Delivering motherhood: Maternal ideologies and practices in the nineteenth and twentieth centuries*. New York: Routledge.

Ashcroft, Bill, Gareth Griffiths, & Helen Tiffin. (Eds.). (1995). *The post-colonial studies reader*. New York: Routledge.

Astin, Helen, & Linda Sax. (1996). Developing scientific talent in undergraduate women. In Cinda Sue Davis, Angela Ginorio, Carol Hollenshead, Barbara Lazarus, & Paula Rayman (Eds.), *The equity equation* (pp. 96–121). San Francisco: Jossey-Bass.

Barros, F. C., J. P. Vaughn, C. G. Victoria, & S. R. A. Huttly. (1991). Epidemic of caesarean sections in Brazil. *Lancet, 2,* 171–175.

Basch, Linda. (1996). Beyond Beijing. *Issues Quarterly, 2*(1), 2–52.

Belenky, Mary Field, Blythe McVicker Clinchy, Nancy Rule Goldberger, & Jill Mattuck Tarule. (1986). *Women's ways of knowing.* New York: Basic Books.

Benbow, Camilla, & J. Stanley. (1984). Gender and the science major. A study of mathematically precocious youth. In M. W. Steinkamp & M. L. Maehr (Eds.), *Women in science* (pp. 425–436). Greenwich, CT: JAI Press.

Bernal, Martin. (1987 & 1991). *Black Athena: The Afroasiatic roots of classical civilization* (Vols. I & II). New Brunswick, NJ: Rutgers University Press.

Bickel, Janet, Kathy Croft, David Johnson, & Renee Marshall. (1997). *Women in U.S. academic medicine: Statistics 1997.* Washington, DC: Association of American Medical Colleges.

Biology and Gender Study Group. (1989). The importance of feminist critique for contemporary cell biology. In Nancy Tuana (Ed.), *Feminism and science* (pp. 172–187). Bloomington: Indiana University Press.

Birke, Lynda. (1986). *Women, feminism, and biology: The feminist challenge.* New York: Methuen.

Bleier, Ruth. (1979). Social and political bias in science: An examination of animal studies and their generalizations to human behavior and evolution. In Ruth Hubbard & Marian Lowe (Eds.), *Genes and gender II: Pitfalls in research on sex and gender* (pp. 49–70). New York: Gordian Press.

Bleier, Ruth. (1984). *Science and gender: A critique of biology and its theories on women.* New York: Pergamon Press.

Bleier, Ruth. (1986). Sex differences research: Science or belief? In Ruth Bleier (Ed.), *Feminist approaches to science* (pp. 147–164). New York: Pergamon Press.

Blum, Elissa. (1993). Making biodiversity conservation profitable: A case study of the Merck/INBio Agreement. *Environment, 35,* 16–20, 38–45.

Blumenstyk, Goldie. (1998, December 4). Berkeley joins Swiss company in controversial technology-transfer pact. *Chronicle of Higher Education,* p. A38.

Boserup, Ester. (1970). *Woman's role in economic development.* New York: St. Martin's Press.

Boston Women's Health Book Collective. (1973). *Our bodies, ourselves* (rev. & exp. 1978, 1984, 1992, 1998). New York: Simon & Schuster.

Boswell, S. (1979, April). *Nice girls don't study mathematics: The perspective from elementary school.* Paper presented at the annual meeting of the American Educational Research Association, San Francisco.

Brandt, Steven, Anita Spring, Clifton Hiebsch, J. T. McCabe, Endale Tabogie, Mulugeta Diro, Gizachew Wolde-Michael, Gebre Yntiso, Masayoshi Shigeta, & Shiferaw Tesfaye. (1997). *The tree against hunger.* Washington, DC: American Association for the Advancement of Science.

Brush, Stephen G. (1991). Women in science and engineering. *American Scientist, 79,* 404–419.

Bukh, Jette. (1979). *The village woman in Ghana.* Uppsala: Scandinavian Institute of African Studies.

Butler, Judith. (1990). *Gender trouble: Feminism and the subversion of identity.* New York: Routledge.

Butler, Judith. (1992). Introduction. In J. Butler & J. Scott (Eds.), *Feminists theorize the political* (pp. xii–xvii). New York: Routledge.

Butler, Judith. (1994). *Bodies that matter: On the discursive limits of "sex."* New York: Routledge.

Campbell, Paulette W. (1998a, July 17). NIH urged to seek public's views on priorities for spending. *Chronicle of Higher Education,* p. A44.

Campbell, Paulette W. (1998b, May 22). Private company's plan creates a doubt about U.S. project on human genome. *Chronicle of Higher Education,* pp. A38–39.

Campbell, Paulette W. (1998c, May 29). US proposes new rules on research subjects. *Chronicle of Higher Education,* p. A35.

CARASA (Committee for Abortion Rights and Against Sterilization Abuse). (1979). *Women under attack: Abortion, sterilization and reproductive freedom.* New York: Author.

Carr, Thomas A., Heather L. Pedersen, & Sunder Ramaswamy. (1993). Rain forest entrepreneurs. *Environment, 35,* 12–15, 33–38.

Center for Women in Government. (1998). *United States Women's leadership profile compendium report.* Albany: State University of New York Press.

Centers for Disease Control. (1980). *Surgical sterilization surveillance: Hysterectomy in women aged 15–44, from 1970–1975.* Atlanta: Author.

Chasnoff, Ira J., Harvey J. Landress, & Mark E. Barrett. (1990, April). The prevalence of illicit-drug or alcohol abuse during pregnancy and discrepancies in mandated reporting in Pinellas County, Florida. *New England Journal of Medicine, 26,* 1202.

Chodorow, Nancy. (1978). *The reproduction of mothering: Psychoanalysis and the sociology of gender.* Berkeley & Los Angeles: University of California Press.

Cixous, Helene, & C. Clement. (1986). *The newly born woman.* Minneapolis: University of Minnesota Press.

Collins, Patricia Hill. (1990). *Black feminist thought.* New York: Routledge.

Corea, Gena. (1985). *The mother machine: Reproductive technologies from artificial insemination to artificial wombs.* New York: Harper & Row.

Corea, Gena. (1991). Who may have children and who may not. In H. Patricia Hynes (Ed.), *Reconstructing Babylon* (pp. 70–80). Bloomington: Indiana University Press, 70–80.

Costello, Cynthia, & Anne Stone. (Eds.). (1994). *The American woman 1994–95.* New York: Norton.

Croce, Paul. (1995). *Science and religion in the era of William James.* Chapel Hill: University of North Carolina Press.

Daly, Mary. (1978). *Gyn/Ecology: The metaethics of radical feminism.* Boston: Beacon Press.

Daly, Mary. (1984). *Pure lust: Elemental feminist philosophy.* Boston: Beacon Press.

Dan, Alice. (Ed.). (1994). *Reframing women's health.* Thousand Oaks, CA: Sage Press.

Davison, Jean. (1988). Land and women's agriculture: The context. In J. Davison

(Ed.), *Agriculture, women and land: The African experience*. Boulder, CO: West-view Press.

Dinnerstein, Dorothy. (1977). *The mermaid and the minotaur: Sexual arrangements and human malaise*. New York: Harper Colophon Books.

Dworkin, Andrea. (1983). *Right-wing women*. New York: Coward-McCann.

Eccles, Jacquelynne S. (1987). Gender roles and women's achievement—related decisions. *Psychology of Women Quarterly, 11*, 135–172.

Eccles, Jacquelynne S., & R. D. Harold. (1992). Gender differences in educational and occupational patterns among the gifted. In N. Colangelo, S. G. Assou-line, & D. L. Ambroson (Eds.), *Talent development: Proceedings from the 1991 Henry B. and Jocelyn Wallace National Research Symposium on Talent Development* (pp. 3–29). Unionville, NY: Trillium Press.

Eccles, Jacquelynne. (1994). Understanding women's educational and occupational choices. *Psychology of Women Quarterly, 11*, 3–29.

Eccles, Jacquelynne, Bonnie Barber, & D. M. Jozefowicz. (1997, April). *Linking gender to educational, occupational, and recreational choices: Applying the Eccles et al. model of achievement—related choices*. Address given at Janet Spence's Festschrift, Austin.

Ehrenreich, Barbara, & Deirdre English. (1978). *For her own good*. New York: Anchor Press.

Elders, Joycelyn M. (1997). In Susan Ambrose, Kristin Dunkle, Barbara Lazarus, Indira Nair, & Deborah Harkus (Eds.), *Journeys of women in science and engi-neering: No universal constants* (pp. 131–134). Philadelphia: Temple University Press.

Engber, Diane. (1996). Evolving a course on postcolonial writings by women. *NWSA Journal, 8*(1), 157–170.

Eschen, Andrea, & Maxine Whittaker. (1993). Family planning: A base to build on for women's reproductive health services. In Marge Koblinsky, Judith Timyan, & Jill Goy (Eds.), *The health of women: A global perspective* (pp. 105–131). Boulder, CO: Westview Press.

Fader, S. (1990, February). Targeting companies that promote women.

Faludi, Susan. (1996). *Backlash*. New York: Crown.

Fausto-Sterling, Anne. (1992). *Myths of gender*. New York: Basic Books.

Fee, Elizabeth. (1982). A feminist critique of scientific objectivity. *Science for the People, 14*(4), 27–33.

Fee, Elizabeth. (1983). Women's nature and scientific objectivity. In Marian Lowe & Ruth Hubbard (Eds.), *Women's nature: Rationalizations of inequality* (pp. 9–27). New York: Pergamon Press.

Flexner, Abraham. (1910). *Medical education in the US and Canada: A report to the Carnegie Foundation for the Advancement of Teaching*. New York: Carnegie Foundation. (Reprinted New York: Arno, 1972)

Fox, L. H., S. R. Pasternak, & N. L. Peiser. (1976). Career-related interests of adolescent boys and girls. In D. P. Keating (Ed.), *Intellectual talent: Re-search and development*. Baltimore: Johns Hopkins University Press.

Gillespie, Marcia Ann. (1998). Norplant is back in Bangladesh. *MS, 9*(1), 32.

Good Maust, Marcia. (1994). The midwife or the knife: The discourse of childbirth by cesarean in Mérida, Yucatán. *Latinamericanist, 30*(1), 1, 7–11.

Good Maust, Marcia. (1996, November). Personal communication of data presented in science and gender class at University of Florida, Gainesville.

Greenberg, Daniel. (1999, March 26). Scientists attack the federal budget with the politics of calculated panic. *Chronicle of Higher Education,* p. A72.

Griffin, Susan. (1978). *The death of nature.* New York: Harper & Row.

Guillette, Elizabeth. (1997). Environmental factors and the health of women. In Sue V. Rosser & Leslie Sue Lieberman (Eds.), *Women's health and research: Multidisciplinary models for excellence.* Gainesville, FL: Custom Copies.

Gumperz, John. (1982). *Language and social identity.* Cambridge, England: Cambridge University Press.

Gunew, Sneja. (1990). *Feminist knowledge: Critique and construct.* New York: Routledge.

Gurwitz, Jerry, F. Colonel Nananda, & Jerry Avorn. (1992). The exclusion of the elderly and women from clinical trials in acute myocardial infarction. *Journal of the American Medical Association, 268*(2), 1407–1422.

Hale, Sondra. (1998). Some comments on conditions for women in revolutionary movements, global and local, with reference to Sudan. In *The role of the Sudanese women in building the new Sudan* [On-line]. Available: WWID-FELLOWS-LOLISTS.UFL.EDU.

Hales, Stuart. (1998). It's the vote that matters. *Outlook, 92*(3), 4–9.

Hall, Roberta, & Bernice Sandler. (1982). *The classroom climate: A chilly one for women.* Washington, DC: Project on the Status and Education for Women, Association of American Colleges.

Haraway, Donna. (1978). Animal sociology and a natural economy of the body politic. *Signs, 4*(1), 21–60.

Haraway, Donna. (1989). *Primate visions: Gender, race, and nature in the world of modern science.* New York: Routledge.

Haraway, Donna. (1992). The promises of monsters: A regenerative politics for inappropriate/d Others. In L. Grossberg, C. Nelson, & P. Treichler (Eds.), *Cultural studies* (pp. 295–337). New York: Routledge.

Haraway, Donna. (1997). *Modest_witness @ second_millennium: Female man©_ meets_oncomouse*™. New York: Routledge.

Harding, Sandra. (1986). *The science question in feminism.* Ithaca, NY: Cornell University Press.

Harding, Sandra. (1991). *Whose science? Whose knowledge?* Ithaca, NY: Cornell University Press.

Harding, Sandra. (1993). Introduction. In Sandra Harding (Ed.), *The racial economy of science* (pp. 1–22). Bloomington: Indiana University Press.

Harding, Sandra. (1998). *Is science multicultural? Postcolonialisms, feminisms, and epistemologies.* Bloomington: Indiana University Press.

Harris, J. R., M. E. Lippman, U. Veronesi, & W. Willett. (1992). Breast cancer. *New England Journal of Medicine, 327,* 319–328.

Hedges, Elaine. (1997). Editorial: Looking back. *Women's Studies Quarterly, XXV*(1–2), 6–13.

Hein, Hilde. (1981). Women and science: Fitting men to think about nature. *International Journal of Women's Studies, 4,* 369–377.

Herz, Diane E., & Barbara E. Wooten. (1996). Women in the workforce: An overview. In Cynthia Costello & Barbara K. Kringold (Eds.), *The American Woman, 1996–97.* New York: Norton.

Hewitt, Nancy. (1997). *US History: Discipline Analysis: Women in the Curriculum.* Baltimore: National Center for Curriculum Transformation Resources on Women.

Hoffman, Joan. (1982). Biorhythms in human reproduction: The not-so-steady states. *Signs, 7*(4), 829–844.

Holmes, Helen B. (1981). Reproductive technologies: The birth of women-centered analysis. In Helen B. Holmes et al. (Eds.), *The custom-made child.* Clifton, NJ: Humana Press.

Holmes, Helen B. (1996, May 16–19). *Women and genetics in contemporary society* (WAG-ICS). Workshop at Muskingum Valley Conference Center, Zanesville, OH.

Holmes, Helen B. (1998). The human genome project and the future of health care. *Academic Medicine, 72*(12), 1123–1125.

Hubbard, Ruth. (1979). Introduction. In Ruth Hubbard & Marian Lowe (Eds.), *Genes and gender II: Pitfalls in research on sex and gender* (pp. 9–34). New York: Gordian Press.

Hubbard, Ruth. (1983). Reflections on the story of the double helix. In Laurel Richardson & Verta Taylor (Eds.), *Feminist frontiers* (pp. 136–144). Reading, MA: Addison Wesley.

Hubbard, Ruth. (1990). *The politics of women's biology.* New Brunswick, NJ: Rutgers University Press.

Hubbard, Ruth. (1995). *Profitable promises: Essays on women, science, and health.* Monroe, ME: Common Courage Press.

Jacobson, Jodi. (1993). Women's health: The price of poverty. In Marge Koblinsky, Judith Timyan, & Jill Gay (Eds.), *The health of women: A global perspective* (pp. 3–32). Boulder, CO: Westview Press.

Jaggar, Alison. (1983). *Feminist politics and human nature.* Totowa, NJ: Rowman & Allanheld.

Jaggar, Alison, & Paula Rothenberg (Eds.). (1992). *Feminist frameworks.* New York: McGraw-Hill.

Jones, Delores. (1998). Memo to mothers at work: Stop feeling guilty! *MS, IX*(1), 40–43.

Jones, James H. (1981). *Bad blood: The Tuskegee syphilis experiment—A tragedy of race and medicine.* New York: Free Press.

Jozefowicz, Deborah M., Bonnie L. Barber, & Jacquelynne S. Eccles. (1993, March). *Adolescent work-related values and beliefs: Gender differences and relation to occupational aspirations.* Paper presented at biennial meeting of the Society for Research on Child Development, New Orleans.

Keller, Evelyn F. (1982). Feminism and science. *Signs, 7*(3), 589–602.

Keller, Evelyn F. (1983). *A feeling for the organism.* San Francisco: Freeman.

Keller, Evelyn F. (1985). *Reflections on gender and science.* New Haven: Yale University Press.

Kelsey, Sheryl F., et al., & Investigators from the National Heart, Lung, and Blood Institute Percutaneous Transluminal Coronary Angioplasty Registry. (1993). Results of percutaneous transluminal coronary angioplasty in women: 1985–1986. *Circulation, 87*(3), 720–727.

King, Jonathan, & Doreen Stabinsky. (1999, February 5). Patents on cells, genes, and organisms undermine the exchange of scientific ideas. *The Chronicle of Higher Education*, pp. B6–7.

King, Mary-Claire, Sara Rowell, & Susan M. Love. (1993, April 21). Inherited breast and ovarian cancer: What are the risks? What are the choices? *Journal of the American Medical Association, 269*, 1975–1980.

King, Ynestra. (1983). Toward an ecological feminism and feminist ecology. In J. Rothschild (Ed.), *Machina ex dea: Feminist perspectives on technology* (pp. 118–129). Elmsford, NY: Pergamon Press.

King, Ynestra. (1989). The ecology of feminism and the feminism of ecology. In J. Plant (Ed.), *Healing the wounds: The promise of ecofeminism* (pp. 18–28). Philadelphia: New Society.

Klein, Renate. (1989). Resistance: From the exploitation of infertility to the exploration of in-fertility. In Renate Klein (Ed.), *Infertility* (pp. 229–295). London: Pandora Press.

Koblinsky, Marge, Judith Timyan, & Jill Gay. (1993). *The health of women: A global perspective.* Boulder, CO: Westview Press.

Kristeva, Julia. (1984). *The revolution in poetic language.* New York: Columbia University Press.

Kristeva, Julia. (1987). *Tales of love.* New York: Columbia University Press.

Lederman, Douglas. (1998, May 29). Senate raises cap on foreign visas. *Chronicle of Higher Education*, p. A35.

Lerner, Sharon. (1996). The price of eggs: Undercover in the infertility industry. *MS, VI*(5), 28–34.

Love, Susan. (1997). Susan Love. In Susan Ambrose, Kristin Dunkle, Barbara Lazarus, Indira Nair, & Deborah Harkus (Eds.), *Journeys of women in science and engineering: No universal constants* (pp. 263–266). Philadelphia: Temple University Press.

MacKinnon, Catharine. (1982). Feminism, Marxism, and the state: An agenda for theory. *Signs, 7*(3), 515–544.

MacKinnon, Catharine. (1987). *Feminism unmodified: Discourses on life and law.* Cambridge, MA: Harvard University Press.

Maines, D. R. (1983, April). *A theory of informal barriers for women in mathematics.* Paper presented at annual meeting of the American Educational Research Association, Montreal.

Matyas, Marsha, & Shirley Malcom. (1991). *Investing in human potential: Science and engineering at the crossroads.* Washington, DC: American Association for the Advancement of Science.

McIntosh, Peggy. (1984). The study of women: Processes of personal and curricular re-vision. *Forum for Liberal Education, 6*(5), 2–4.

Merchant, Carolyn. (1979). *The death of nature.* New York: Harper & Row.

Miller, David W., & Robin Wilson. (1999, April 2). MIT acknowledges bias against female faculty members. *Chronicle of Higher Education*, p. A18.

Miller, Patricia H., Sue V. Rosser, Joann Benigno, & Mireille Zieseniss. (in press). A desire to help others: Goals of high achieving female science undergraduates. *Women's Studies Quarterly*.

Mohanty, Chandra T. (1984). Under Western eyes: Feminist scholarship and colonial discourses. *Boundary 2, 12*(3) & *13*(1).

Mohanty, Chandra T. (1997). Women workers and capitalist scripts: Ideologies of domination, common interests, and the politics of solidarity. In M. Jacqui Alexander & Chandra T. Mohanty (Eds.), *Feminist genealogies, colonial legacies, democratic futures*. New York: Routledge.

Mooney, Carolyn. (1998, September 11). An ethnobotanist and a shaman explore the power and promise of medicinal plants. *Chronicle of Higher Education*, p. B2.

Morantz-Sanchez, Regina. (1988). *Sympathy and science*. New York: Oxford University Press.

Moses, Yolanda. (1995, November 17). *The international women's movement in the US and beyond: 20 years and beyond*. Paper delivered at the ninety-fourth meeting of the American Anthropological Association, Washington, DC.

Muller, Charlotte F. (1992). *Healthcare and gender*. New York: Russell Sage Foundation.

Mulligan, Joan E. (1992). Nursing and feminism: Caring and curing. In Chris Kramarae & Dale Spender (Eds.), *The knowledge explosion*. New York: Teachers College Press.

National Science Board. (1996). *Science & engineering indicators—1996* (NSB 96–21). Washington, DC: U.S. Government Printing Office.

National Science Foundation. (1992). *Women and minorities in science and engineering: An update* (NSF 92–303). Washington, DC: Author.

National Science Foundation, Division of Science Resource Studies. (1997a). *Science and engineering degrees: 1966–95* (NSF 97–335), by Susan T. Hill. Arlington, VA: U.S. Government Printing Office.

National Science Foundation, Division of Science Resource Studies. (1997b). *Science and engineering doctorate awards: 1996* Detailed Statistical Tables (NSF 97–329), by Susan T. Hill. Arlington, VA: U.S. Government Printing Office.

Nayar, Javed. (1996, September 26–28). *Women as racialized faces in science*. Presented at the conference, Women and Other Faces in Sciences, University of Saskatchewan, Saskatoon.

Needham, Joseph. (1969). Poverties and triumphs of the Chinese scientific tradition. *The grand titration*. Toronto: University of Toronto Press.

Needham, Joseph, with Wang Ling (Wang Ching-Ning), Lu Gwei-Djen, Ho Ping-Yu, Kenneth Robinson, Tshao Thein-Chhin, & others. (1954). *Science and civilization in China* (Vols. 1–7). Cambridge, England: Cambridge University Press.

Noddings, Nel. (1984). *Caring: A feminine approach to ethics and moral caring*. Berkeley: University of California Press.

O'Brien, Mary. (1981). *The politics of reproduction*. Boston: Routledge & Kegan Paul.

Pehu, Eija, & Mary Rojas. (1997). Food security, environmental issues and human health: A potential with biotechnology and plant genetic resources with economic, social and political views. In Kazuo N. Watanabe & Eija Pehu (Eds.), *Plant biotechnology and plant genetic resources for sustainability and productivity* (pp. 15–20). New York: R. J. Landes.

Pinn, Vivian, & Judith LaRosa. (1992). *Overview: Office of research on women's health.* Bethesda, MD: National Institutes of Health.

Prince: Leave food making to God. (1998, June 9). *The Gainesville Sun*, p. A2.

Radcliffe Public Policy Institute. (1996). *Work, family, and community, facts at a glance.* Cambridge, MA: Radcliffe Public Policy Institute.

Raymond, Janice. (1991). In the matter of Baby M: Judged and rejudged. In H. Patricia Hynes (Ed.), *Reconstructing Babylon.* Bloomington: Indiana University Press.

Rich, Adrienne. (1976). *Of woman born: Motherhood as experience.* New York: Norton.

Rodriguez, Evelyn M. (1997).In Susan Ambrose, Kristin Dunkle, Barbara Lazarus, Indira Nair, & Deborah Harkus (Eds.), *Journeys of women in science and engineering: No universal constants* (pp. 319–322). Philadelphia: Temple University Press.

Rose, Hilary. (1983). Hand, brain, and heart: A feminist epistemology for the natural sciences. *Signs, 9*(1), 73–90.

Rose, Hilary. (1994). *Love, power, and knowledge: Towards a feminist transformation of the sciences.* Bloomington: Indiana University Press.

Rosser, Sue V. (1982). Androgyny and sociobiology. *International Journal of Women's Studies, 5*(5), 435–444.

Rosser, Sue V. (1986). *Teaching science and health from a feminist perspective: A practical guide.* New York: Pergamon Press.

Rosser, Sue V. (1988). Women in science and health care: A gender at risk. In Sue V. Rosser (Ed.), *Feminism within the science and health care professions: Overcoming resistance* (pp. 3–15). New York: Pergamon Press.

Rosser, Sue V. (1990). *Female friendly science.* New York: Pergamon Press.

Rosser, Sue V. (1992). *Biology & feminism: A dynamic interaction.* New York: Twayne.

Rosser, Sue V. (1993). Female friendly science: Including women in curricular content and pedagogy in science. *The Journal of General Education, 42*(3), 191–220.

Rosser, Sue V. (1994). *Women's health: Missing from U.S. medicine.* Bloomington: Indiana University Press.

Rosser, Sue V. (1995). *Teaching the majority.* New York: Teachers College Press.

Rosser, Sue V. (1997a). *Re-engineering female friendly science.* New York: Teachers College Press.

Rosser, Sue V. (1997b). The millennium is here now: Women's studies perspectives on biotechnics and reproductive technologies. *Transformations, 8*(1), 1–27.

Rosser, Sue V. (1998). The next millennium is now here: Women's studies perspectives on biotechnics and reproductive technologies. In Boel Berner (Ed.), *New perspectives in gender studies: Research in the fields of economics, culture and life sciences* (pp. 7–35). Stockholm, Sweden: Almquist and Wilosell International.

Rosser, Sue V., & Mireille Zieseniss. (1999). *Different challenges and opportunities: Women engineers and scientists.* In Barbara Bogue, Priscilla Guthrie, Barbara

Lazarus, & Steve Hadden (Eds.), *Tackling the engineering resources shortage. Proceedings of an International Engineering Foundation Conference* (pp. 64–72). Bellingham, WA: International Society for Optical Engineering.

Rossiter, Margaret W. (1984). *Women scientists in America: Struggles and strategies to 1940.* Baltimore: Johns Hopkins University Press.

Rossiter, Margaret W. (1995). *Women scientists in America: Before affirmative action 1940–1972.* Baltimore: Johns Hopkins University Press.

Rothfield, Philipa. (1990). Feminism, subjectivity, and sexual difference. In Sneja Gunew (Ed.), *Feminist knowledge: Critique and construct* (pp. 121–144). New York: Routledge.

Sagraves, Ruth. (Ed.). (1995, September). Women's health research issues. *American Pharmacy*, n.s., *35* (Suppl. 9), S1–S11.

Said, Edward. (1978). *Orientalism.* New York: Random House.

Saxton, Marsha. (1996). Disability rights and selective abortion in the fifty years war. In Ricki Solinger (Ed.), *Abortion politics, 1950–2000.* Berkeley: University of California Press.

Sayre, Anne. (1975). *Rosalind Franklin and DNA.* New York: Norton.

Schuster, Marilyn, & Susan Van Dyne. (1984). Placing women in the liberal arts: Stages of curriculum transformation. *Harvard Educational Review, 54*(4), 413–428.

Seymour, Elaine, & Nancy Hewitt. (1994). *Talking about leaving: Factors contributing to high attrition rates among science, mathematics, and engineering undergraduate majors.* Boulder, CO: Ethnography and Assessment Research, Bureau of Sociological Research.

Shattuck-Edens, D., M. McClure, J. Simard, et al. (1995). A collaborative survey of 80 mutations in BRCA-1 breast and ovarian cancer susceptibility genes: Implications for pre-symptomatic testing and screening. *Journal of the American Medical Association, 273*(7), 535–541.

Shiva, Vandana. (1989). *Staying alive: Women, ecology, and development.* London: Zed Books.

Shiva, Vandana. (1991a). *Ecology and the politics of survival: Conflicts over natural resources in India.* New Delhi: United Nations University Press & Sage.

Shiva, Vandana. (1991b). The seed and the spinning wheel. In Shiva, *The violence of the green revolution: Third world agriculture, ccology, and politics.* London: Zed Books.

Shiva, Vandana. (1997). *Biopiracy: The plunder of nature and knowledge.* Boston: South End Press.

Silbergeld, Ellen Kovner. (1997). In Susan Ambrose, Kristin Dunkle, Barbara Lazarus, Indira Nair, & Deborah Harkus (Eds.), *Journeys of women in science and engineering: No universal constants* (pp. 361–362). Philadelphia: Temple University Press.

Soto, A. M., C. Sonnenschein, K. L. Chung, M. F. Fernandez, N. Olea, & F. Olea Serano. (1995). The e-screen assay as a tool to identify estrogens: An update on estrogenic environmental pollutants. *Environmental Health Perspectives, 103*(Suppl. 7), 113–122.

Spanier, Bonnie. (1982, April). Toward a balanced curriculum: The study of women at Wheaton College. *Change, 14,* 31–34.

Spivak, Gayatri Chakravorty. (1985). Three women's texts and a critique of imperialism. *Critical Inquiry, 12*(1), 262–280.

Spivak, Gayatri Chakravorty. (1988). Can the subaltern speak? In Cary Nelson & Lawrence Grossberg (Eds.), *Marxism and the interpretation of culture* (pp. 271–313). London: Macmillan.

Spring, Anita. (1995). *Agricultural development and gender issues in Malawi.* New York: University Press of America.

Starr, Cecil, & Ralph Taggart. (1984). *Biology: The unity and diversity of life* (3rd ed.). Belmont, CA: Wadsworth.

Steering Committee of the Physician's Health Study Group. (1989). Final report of the aspirin component of the ongoing Physician's Health Study. *New England Journal of Medicine, 3221,* 129–135.

Subramanian, Banu. (in press). Snow Brown and the seven detergents. *Women's Studies Quarterly.*

Suleri, Sara. (1992, Summer). Woman skin deep: Feminism and the postcolonial condition. *Critical Inquiry, 18*(4), 756–769.

Sullivan, Deborah, & Rose Weitz. (1988). *Labor pains: Modern midwives and home birth.* New Haven: Yale University Press.

Tanesini, A. (1999). *An introduction to feminist epistemologies.* Oxford: Blackwell.

Tannen, Deborah. (1990). *You just don't understand.* New York: Morrow.

Teraguchi, Sonja. (1997). In Susan Ambrose, Kristin Dunkle, Barbara Lazarus, Indira Nair, & Deborah Harkus (Eds.), *Journeys of women in science and engineering: No universal constants* (pp. 390–394). Philadelphia: Temple University Press.

Tetreault, Mary Kay. (1985). Stages of thinking about women: An experience-derived evaluation model. *Journal of Higher Education, 5,* 368–384.

Thiong'o, Ngugi Wa. (1972). On the abolition of the English department. In Thiong'o, *Homecoming: Essays on African and Caribbean literature, culture and politics.* London: Heinemann.

Tong, Rosemarie. (1989). *Feminist thought: A comprehensive introduction.* Boulder, CO: Westview Press.

Tuana, Nancy. (1989). The weaker seed: The sexist bias of reproductive theory. In Nancy Tuana (Ed.), *Feminism and science* (pp. 147–171). Bloomington: Indiana University Press.

Usher, Ann Danaiya. (1994). After the forest: AIDS as ecological collapse in Thailand. In Vandana Shiva (Ed.), *Close to home: Women reconnect ecology, health and development worldwide* (pp. 10–42). Philadelphia and Gabriola Island, BC: New Society.

U.S. General Accounting Office. (1990, June 19). *National Institutes of Health: Problems in implementing policy on women in study populations.* Statement of Mark V. Nadel, Associate Director, National and Public Health Issues, Human Resources Division, before the Subcommittee on Health and the Environment, Committee on Energy and Commerce, U.S. House of Representatives.

Vetter, Betty. (1988). Where are the women in the physical sciences? In Sue V. Rosser (Ed.), *Feminism within the science and health care professions: Overcoming resistance* (pp. 19–32). New York: Pergamon Press.

Vetter, Betty. (1992). *What is holding up the glass ceiling? Barriers to women in the science and engineering workforce* (Occasional paper 92–3). Washington, DC: Commission on Professionals in Science and Technology.

Vetter, Betty. (1996). Women in science, mathematics and engineering: Myths and realities. In Cinda-Sue Davis, Angela B. Ginorio, Carol S. Hollenshead, Barbara B. Lazarus, Paula M. Rayman, & Associates (Eds.), *The equity equation: Fostering the advancement of women in the sciences, mathematics, and engineering.* San Francisco: Jossey-Bass.

Viswanathan, Gauri. (1987). The beginnings of English literary study in British India. *Oxford Literary Review, 9*(1&2), 2–26.

Wallis, Lila A. (1981). Advancement of men and women in medical academia. *Journal of the American Medical Women's Association, 246*(20), 2350–2353.

Washburn, Jennifer. (1996). The misuses of Norplant: Who gets stuck? *MS, VII*(3), 32–36.

Watson, James D. (1969). *The double helix.* New York: Atheneum.

Weatherford, Jack. (1988). *Indian givers.* New York: Crown.

Weatherford, Jack. (1993). Early Andean experimental agriculture. In Sandra Harding (Ed.), *The "racial" economy of science* (pp. 64–77). Bloomington: Indiana University Press.

Wertz, Richard, & Dorothy Wertz. (1977). *Lying-in: A history of childbirth in America.* New York: Free Press.

Wheeler, David. (1998). Human genome project plans to speed work. *Chronicle of Higher Education, 45*(5), A20.

Williams, Patrick, & Laura Chrisman. (1994). Colonial discourse and post-colonial theory: An introduction. In Patrick Williams & Laura Chrisman (Eds.), *Colonial discourse and post-colonial theory* (pp. 1–20). New York: Columbia University Press.

Wolfson, Nessa. (1989). *Perspectives: Sociolinguistics and TESOL.* Towley, MA: Newbury.

Women's Community Cancer Project. (1992, Fall). A woman's cancer agenda: The demands. *Women's Community Cancer Project Newsletter, 2,* 2.

Women's Community Cancer Project. (1994, Winter). National Breast Cancer Coalition. *Women's Community Cancer Project Newsletter, 4,* 4.

Wright, Alexi. (1998, Summer). Xeno: Tapping the animal organ bank. *Academy Update: New York Academy of Sciences Member Newsletter, 1,* 7–16.

Zimmerman, Bill et al. (1980). People's science. In Rita Arditti, Pat Brennan, & Steve Cavrak (Eds.), *Science and liberation* (pp. 299–319). Boston: South End Press.

Selected Bibliography on Feminism and Science

Compiled by Faye A. Chadwell

Abir-Am, P. G., & Outram, D. (Eds.). (1987). *Uneasy careers and intimate lives: Women in science, 1787–1979.* New Brunswick, NJ: Rutgers University Press.

Abraham, I. (1998). *The making of the Indian atomic bomb: Science, secrecy and the postcolonial state.* New York: Zed Books.

Adams, C. J. (1991, May–June). Anima, animus, animal (Animal rights and feminism are compatible). *Ms. Magazine, 1*(6), 62–63.

Adams, C. J. (1991, Spring). Ecofeminism and the eating of animals. *Hypatia, 6*(1), 125–145.

Adams, C. J., & Donovan, J. (Eds.). (1995). *Animals and women: Feminist theoretical explorations.* Durham, NC: Duke University Press.

Affirmative inaction? (1995). *The Scientist, 9*(14), 1.

African women need to have access to education and employment in science and technology. (1995, January). *Femnet News, 5*(1), 9.

Afshar, H., & Maynard, M. (1994). *The dynamics of "race" and gender: Some feminist interventions.* Bristol, PA: Taylor & Francis.

Agarwal, B. (1998). Environmental management, equity and ecofeminism: Debating India's experience. *The Journal of Peasant Studies, 25*(4), 55–95.

Alaimo, S. (1994, Spring). Cyborg and ecofeminist interventions: Challenges for an environmental feminism. *Feminist Studies, 20*(1), 133–152.

Alarcon, N. (Ed.). (1993). *Chicana critical issues.* Berkeley: Third Woman Press.

Alcoff, L. M. (1998, Summer). What should white people do? (Combatting racism) [Special issue: Border crossings: Multicultural and postcolonial feminist challenges to philosophy, part 2]. *Hypatia, 13*(3), 6–26.

Ambrose, S., Dunkle, K., Lazarus, B., Nair, I., & Harkus, D. (Eds.). (1997). *Journeys of women in science and engineering: No universal constants.* Philadelphia: Temple University Press.

Antony, L. M., & Witt, C. (Eds.). (1993). *A mind of one's own: Feminist essays on reason and objectivity.* Boulder, CO: Westview Press.

Apple, R. D. (Ed.). (1990). *Women, health, and medicine in America: A historical handbook*. New York: Garland.

Arditti, R., Klein R. D., & Minden, S. (Eds.). (1984). *Test-tube women*. London: Pandora Press.

Arnhart, L. (1995, August). Nature and culture in feminist biology. *Politics and the Life Sciences*, pp. 163–164.

Assessing the climate for women. (1994, January 10). *The Scientist, 8*(1), 1.

Assisted reproduction: Where bioethics and gender meet. (1997, April–June). *Women's Health Journal*, pp. 44–46.

Baer, D. L. (1990). Sex/gender/male–female: Science or scientific myth. *Journal of Social and Biological Structures, 13*(4), 411–416.

Bahri, D. (1995, January). Once more with feeling: What is postcolonialism? *ARIEL, 26*(1), 51–82.

Baker, D. K. (1998, Summer). Dualisms, discourse, and development. [Special issue: Border crossings: Multicultural and postcolonial feminist challenges to philosophy, part 2]. *Hypatia, 13*(3), 83–94.

Barber, L. A. (1995, March). U.S. women in science and engineering, 1960–1990: Progress toward equity? *The Journal of Higher Education, 66*(2), 213.

Bari, J. (1992, May/June). Feminization of earth first. *Ms. Magazine, 2*(6), 84–85.

Barker, F., Hulme, P., & Iversen, M. (Eds.). (1994). *Colonial discourse/postcolonial theory*. New York: St. Martin's Press.

Barr, J., & Birke, L. (1995). Cultures and contexts of adult learners: The case of women and science. *Studies in the Education of Adults, 27*(2), 119–132.

Barroso, C. (1993, July–September). The alliance between feminists and researchers: Meeting women's unmet needs. *Women's Health Journal*, no. 3, 4–11.

Bartels, D. M. (Ed.). (1990). *Beyond Baby M: Ethical issues in new reproductive techniques*. Clifton, NJ: Humana Press.

Barton, A. C. (1998). *Feminist science education*. New York: Teachers College Press.

Bauman, E. (1998, Autumn). Re-dressing colonial discourse: Postcolonial theory and the Humanist Project. *Critical Quarterly, 40*(3), 79–89.

Bauman, R. (1988). Effects of racism in the technology and science of human reproduction control. *Feminists in Science and Technology, 1*(2), 8–11.

Beauchamp, R. S., & Avedon, L. (1991, Fall). Transforming the science curriculum/ A changer: Le programme de sciences. *Women's Education/Education des Femmes, 9*(2), 2–3.

Before it's too late. (1990, October 15). *The Scientist, 4*(20), 1.

Behuniak-Long, S. (1990). Radical conceptions: Reproductive technologies and feminist theories. *Women & Politics, 10*(3), 39–64.

Bell, S. E. (1994, January–February). Translating science to the people: Updating the new *Our Bodies, Ourselves. Women's Studies International Forum, 17*(1), 9–18.

Bell, S. E. (1995). Gendered medical science: Producing a drug for women. *Feminist Studies, 21*(3), 469–500.

Bellisari, A. (1991, June). Cultural influences on the science career choices of women. *Ohio Journal of Science, 91*(3), 129.

Benjamin, M. (Ed.). (1993). *A question of identity: Women, science, and literature.* New Brunswick, NJ: Rutgers University Press.

Benjamin, M. (Ed.).(1994). *Science and sensibility: Gender and scientific enquiry, 1780–1945.* Cambridge, MA: Basil Blackwell.

Berner, B. (Ed.). (1997). *Gendered practices: Feminist studies of technology and society.* Linkoping, Sweden: Linkoping University, Department of Technology and Social Change.

Bhansali, K. H. (1996). Science and technology in the service of women. *Economic and Political Weekly, 31*(16–17), WS42.

Bias charged. (1994, January 10). *The Scientist, 8*(1), 1.

A bibliography of historical women in science and mathematics. (1994, May). *School Science and Mathematics, 94*(5), 271.

Biehl, J. (1992, Summer). Perspectives on ecofeminism: Viewpoint. *Environmental Action Magazine, 24*(2), 19.

Bindon, K. (1991, Fall). Strange history of a good idea. *Women's Education/Education des Femmes, 9*(2), 11–14.

Bioethics and gender: Subjectivity as a condition of health. (1997, April–June). *Women's Health Journal,* pp. 41–43.

Biology and Gender Study Group. (1988, Spring). Importance of feminist critique for contemporary cell biology. *Hypatia, 3*(1), 61–76.

Bird, S. J., & Didion, C. J. (1992, Fall). Retaining women science students: A mentoring project of the Association for Women in Science. *Initiatives, 55*(3), 3–12.

Birke, L. (1986). *Women, feminism and biology: The feminist challenge.* New York: Methuen.

Birke, L. (1991). Science, feminism, and animal natures II: Feminist critiques and the place of animals in science. *Women's Studies International Forum, 14*(5), 451–458.

Birke, L. (1994). *Feminism, animals, and science: The naming of the shrew.* Philadelphia: Open University Press.

Birke, L. (1995, August). Sociobiology, ideology, and feminism. *Politics and the Life Sciences,* pp. 165–166.

Birke, L., & Barr, J. (1994). Women, science, and adult education: Toward a feminist curriculum? *Women's Studies International Forum, 17*(5), 473–483.

Birke, L., Himmelweit, S., & Vines, G. (1990). *Tomorrow's child: Reproductive technologies in the 90s.* London: Virago.

Birke, L., & Whitworth, R. (1998, March–April). Seeking knowledge: Women, science, and Islam. *Women's Studies International Forum, 21*(2), 147–160.

Birkeland, J. (1995, Winter). Neutralizing gender. *Environmental Ethics, 17*(4), 443–444.

Birkeland, J. (1995). The relevance of ecofeminism to the environmental professions. *The Environmental Professional: The Official Journal of the National Association of Environmental Professionals (NAEP), 17*(1), 55.

Blank, R., & Merrick, J. C. (1995). *Human reproduction, emerging technologies, and conflicting rights.* Washington, DC: CQ Press.

Bleier, R. (1984). *Science and gender: A critique of biology and its theories on women.* New York: Pergamon Press.

Bleier, R. (1988, Autumn). Cultural price of social exclusion: Gender and science. *NWSA Journal, 1*(1), 7–19.

Bleier, R. (1991). *Feminist approaches to science.* New York: Teachers College Press.

Bradish, P. (1991). Het maken van leven—voortplantingstechnologie en genetische manipulatie vanuit het perspectief van een faministische wetenschapskritiek [The construction of life. Reproductive and genetic engineering from the perspective of a feminist critique of science]. *Tijdschrift Voor Vrouwenstudies, 12*(3), 387–403.

Braidotti, R., & Rosi, B. et al. (1994). Women, the environment and sustainable development: Towards a theoretical synthesis. *Theory, Culture & Society, 11*(4), 187.

Brainard, S. G., & Carlin, L. (1997). A longitudinal study of undergraduate women in engineering & science. *Proceedings—Frontiers in Education Conference, 1,* 134–143.

Brattstrom, B. H. (1995). Women in science: Do we ignore female role models? *Bulletin of the Ecological Society of America, 76*(3), 143–151.

Breene, L. A. (1992). Women and computer science. *Initiatives, 55*(2), 39–44.

Brennan, M. (1997, April 28). Women scientists and philosophers: Can we talk? *Chemical and Engineering News, 75*(17), 30.

Brett, A. (1986, March). Biotech is good for women. *Kinesis,* p. 13.

Bridotti, R. (1989, Winter). Organs without bodies. *Differences, 1*(1), 147–161.

Brouwer, C. (1990). Hikrarchie or harmonie? Gender en de wetenschappelijke benadering van de natuur [Hierarchy or harmony? Gender and the scientific approach of nature]. *Tijdschrift Voor Vrouwenstudies, 11*(3), 260–271.

Brown, J., Andreae, P., Biddle, R., & Tempero, E. (1997). Women in introductory computer science: Experience at Victoria University of Wellington. *SIGCSE Bulletin, 29*(1), 111–115.

Brown, R. (1993, Winter). Canada: A new language for the environment. *Connexions,* no. 41, 2–3.

Brush, S. G. (1995). Women, science, and universities. *Bulletin of Science, Technology & Society, 15*(4), 205.

Burda, G. A. (1997, November–December). The battle between political agendas and science. *Skeptical Inquirer, 21*(6), 13.

Burfoot, A. (1987, December). Impediments to feminist acts in science. *Resources for Feminist Research, 16*(4), 25–26.

Byres, T. J. (1998). Chipko, the environment, ecofeminism and populism/neopopulism. *The Journal of Peasant Studies, 25*(4), 33.

Byrne, E. M. (1993). *Women and science: The snark syndrome.* Washington, DC: Falmer Press.

Byrne, E., Brickhouse, N. W., Letts, W. J., & Tan, S. K. (1998). Women and science: The snark syndrome. *Science Education, 82*(2), 285.

Callahan, J. C. (1995). *Reproduction, ethics, and the law: Feminist perspectives.* Bloomington: Indiana University Press.

Campbell, R. (1995, March/April). Weaving a new tapestry of research: A bibliography of selected readings on feminist research methods. *Women's Studies International Forum, 18*(2), 215–222.

Cancian, F. M. (1992). 1991 Cheryl Miller lecture: Feminist science—methodologies that challenge inequality. *Gender & Society, 6*(4), 623–642.

Candib, L. M. (1995). *Medicine and the family: A feminist perspective.* New York: Basic Books.

Caraway, N. (1992, Spring). The cunning of history: Empire, identity and feminist theory in the flesh. (Feminists of color emphasize identity politics). *Women & Politics, 12*(2), 1–18.

Chambers, N. G. (1988, Winter). Feminism and science. *Signs, 13*, 340–343.

Chipman, S. F., Krantz, D. H., & Silver, R. (1992, September). Mathematics anxiety and science careers among able college women. *Psychological Science: A Journal of the American Psychological Society, 3*(5), 292.

Chisholm, J. S. (1995, August). Sociobiology, feminism, and morality. *Politics and the Life Sciences*, pp. 169–170.

Christiansen-Ruffman, L. (1993, Winter). Community base and feminist vision: The essential grounding of science in women's community. *Canadian Woman Studies/Les Cahiers de la Femme 13*(2), 16–20.

Clarke, A. (1998). *Disciplining reproduction: Modernity, American life sciences, and "the problems of sex."* Berkeley: University of California Press.

Clarke, A., & Montini, T. (1993, Winter). The many faces of RU486: Tales of situated knowledges and technological contestations. *Science, Technology, & Human Values, 18*(1), 42–78.

Clarke, A., & Olesen, V. L. (1998). *Revisioning women, health and healing: Feminist, cultural, and technoscience perspectives.* New York: Routledge.

Clewell, B. C., & Anderson, B. (1991). *Women of color in mathematics, science and engineering: A review of the literature.* Washington, DC: Center for Women in Policy Studies.

Clifford, A. M. (1992). Feminist perspectives on science: implications for an ecological theology of creation. *Journal of Feminist Studies in Religion, 8*(2), 65–90.

Cockburn, C., & Ormrod, S. (1993). *Gender and technology in the making.* Thousand Oaks, CA: Sage.

Code, L. (1998, Spring). How to think globally: Stretching the limits of imagination. [Special issue: Border crossings: Multicultural and postcolonial feminist challenges to philosophy, part 1]. *Hypatia, 13*(2), 73–85.

Collins, J., & Rodin, A. (1991). *Women and new reproductive technologies: Medical, psychosocial, legal, and ethical dilemmas.* Hillsdale, NJ: Erlbaum.

Collins, P. H. (1998, Summer). It's all in the family: Intersections of gender, race, and nation. [Special issue: Border crossings: Multicultural and postcolonial feminist challenges to philosophy, part 2]. *Hypatia, 13*(3), 62–82.

Condit, D. M. (1994). Writing reproduction: Reproductive technologies and motherhood examined. *Policy Sciences, 27*(2–3), 287.

Cook, J. (1998). The philosophical colonization of ecofeminism. *Environmental Ethics, 20*(3), 227.

Corea, G. (1985). *The mother machine: Reproductive technologies from artificial insemination to artificial wombs.* New York: Harper & Row.

Corea, G. (Ed.). (1987). *Man-made woman*. Bloomington: Indiana University Press.

Corliss, J. O. (1993). The contributions of women to the science of protozoology. *Acta Protozoologica, 32*(3), 129–134.

Coughlin, E. (1984, July 5). Feminist science foreseen. *Chronicle of Higher Education, 28*, 5.

Coyner, S. (1993, Spring). Feminist research methods. *NWSA Journal, 5*(1), 111–119.

Crouch, M. L. (1995, February). Thinking globally, acting locally. *Women's Review of Books, 12*(5), 32–33.

Cudd, A. E. (1998, Summer). Multiculturalism as a cognitive virtue of scientific practice. [Special issue: Border crossings: Multicultural and postcolonial feminist challenges to philosophy, part 2]. *Hypatia, 13*(3), 43–61.

Cummings, N. B. (1998, March). Biomedical ethics and women's health: Ethical issues and dilemmas. *Journal of Women's Health, 7*(2), 173–176.

Cummings, S. (1996). Mission possible—Representation of women in science. *Chemistry in Australia, 63*(5), 241–245.

Cuomo, C. J. (1992, Winter). Unravelling the problems in ecofeminism. *Environmental Ethics, 14*(4), 351–364.

Currie, K. (1997). Roots of crisis: Interpreting contemporary Indian society/the science of empire: Scientific knowledge, civilization, and colonial rule/the New Cambridge History of India: Women in modern India. *Journal of Contemporary Asia, 27*, 403.

Curtis, K. F. (1995, Winter). Hannah Arendt, feminist theorizing, and the debate over new reproductive technologies. *Polity, 28*, 159–188.

Dagg, A. I., & Beauchamp, R. S. (1991, Spring). Is there a feminist science? Perceived impact of gender on research by women scientists. *Atlantis, 16*, 77–84.

Daie, J. (1994, December). Women in science. *Journal of College Science Teaching, XXIV*(3), 159.

Davis, C. (1996). *The equity equation: Fostering the advancement of women in the sciences, mathematics, and engineering*. San Francisco: Jossey-Bass.

Davis, F. (1996). *La pedagogie feministe en sciences physiques: Compte rendu de recherche*. Saint-Laurent, Quebec: F. Davis.

A death of women in science. (1994, September 14). *The Chronicle of Higher Education, 41*(3), A80.

De Koninck, M. (1986, November). Que serait une approche feministe de la science? *Resources for Feminist Research, 15*(3), 62–64.

Demarco, D. (1992, Winter). The politicization of motherhood. *The Human Life Review, 18*(1), 29–40.

Denora T. (1996, September). From physiology to feminism. Reconfiguring body, gender and expertise in natural fertility control. *International Sociology, 11*(3), 359–383.

Diamond, I. (1994). *Fertile ground: Women, earth, and the limits of control*. Boston: Beacon Press.

Didion, C. J. (1995, Spring). Mentoring women in science. *Educational Horizons, 73*(3), 141.

Do female professors attract more women to science? (1995, April 7). *Chronicle of Higher Education, 41*(30), A16.

Donchin, A. (1986, Fall). The future of mothering: Reproductive technology and feminist theory. *Hypatia, 1*(1), 121–137.

Donchin, A. (1993). *Procreation, power and subjectivity: Feminist approaches to new reproductive technologies.* Wellesley, MA: Center for Research on Women.

Donchin, A. (1996, October). Feminist critiques of new fertility technologies: Implications for social policy. *Journal of Medicine and Philosophy, 21*(5), 475–498.

Donini, E. (1994). Feminisms, contextualization, and diversity: A critical perspective on science and development. *Women's Studies International Forum, 17*(2–3), 249–256.

Dresselhaus, M. S., Franz, J. R., & Clark, B. C. (1994, March 11). Interventions to increase the participation of women in physics. *Science, 263*(11), 1392.

Dumais, L. (1992). Impact of the participation of women in science: On rethinking the place of women especially in occupational health. *Women & Health, 18*(3), 11–26.

Duncan, N. (1996). *Bodyspace: Destabilising geographies of gender and sexuality.* New York: Routledge.

Duster, T., & Garrett, K. (Eds.). (1984). *Cultural perspectives on biological knowledge.* Norwood, NJ: ABLEX.

Ehn, I. (1997, First Semester). Technological dreams and life embracing ethics. *Instraw News,* no. 26, 12–14.

Elshtain, J. B. (1989, June). Technology as destiny. *The Progressive, 53*(6), 19–23.

Elshtain, J. B. (1995, Winter). Exporting feminism. (Transcending national boundaries). *Journal of International Affairs, 48*(2), 541–558.

Emel, J. (1995). Are you man enough, big and bad enough? Ecofeminism and wolf eradication in the USA. *Environment and Planning. D, Society & Space, 13*(6), 707–734.

Encouraging women into science. (1995). *Materials World: The Journal of the Institute of Materials, 3*(8), 370.

Erinosho, S. Y. (1994). Nigerian women in science and technology. *Gender and Education, 6*(2), 201.

Etzkowitz, H., Kemelgor, C., Neuschatz, M., & Uzzi, B. (1992, June). Athena unbound: Barriers to women in academic science and engineering. *Science & Public Policy, 19*(3), 157–179.

Eyes on the ceiling: Top female science policymakers note that more women than ever before are attaining high-level positions; but others contend that barriers to women's advancement still exist. (1997). *The Scientist, 11*(23), 1.

Farquhar, D. (1996). *The other machine: Discourse and reproductive technologies.* New York: Routledge.

Fausto-Sterling, A. (1989). Life in the XY corral. *Women's Studies International Forum, 12*(3), 319–331.

Fausto-Sterling, A. (1992). Building two-way streets: The case of feminism and science. *NWSA Journal, 4*(3), 336–349. (Comments on this essay by S. Harding, R. Hubbard, S. Rosser, & N. Tuana follow in the Spring 1993 issue of *NWSA Journal.* Fausto-Sterling responds to these comments in the same issue.)

Fausto-Sterling, A. (1993, Spring). Response [to comments on her essay "Building two-way streets"]. *NWSA Journal, 5*(1), 77–81.

Fausto-Sterling, A. (1995, August). Attacking feminism is no substitute for good scholarship. *Politics and the Life Sciences*, pp. 171–173.

Fausto-Sterling, A., & Benjamin, M. (1995). A question of identity: Women, science and literature. *Signs, 21*(1), 172–175.

Fedigan, L. M. (1994, September). Science and the successful female: Why there are so many women primatologists. *American Anthropologist, 96*(3), 529.

Fee, E. (1981, September/October). Is feminism a threat to scientific objectivity. *International Journal of Women's Studies, 4*(4), 378–392.

Feenberg, A., & Hannay, A. (1995). *Technology and the politics of knowledge.* Bloomington: Indiana University Press.

Ferguson, A. (1998, Summer). Resisting the veil of privilege: Building bridge identities as an ethico-politics of global feminisms. [Special issue: B order crossings: Multicultural and postcolonial feminist challenges to philosophy, part 2]. *Hypatia, 13*(3), 95–113.

Figueira-Mcdonough, J., & Sani, R. (Eds.). (1987). *The trapped woman.* Newbury Park, CA: Sage.

Fisher, A., Margolis, J., & Miller, F. (1997). Undergraduate women in computer science: Experience, motivation and culture. *SIGCSE Bulletin, 29*(1), 106–110.

Flores-Ortiz, Y. (1993). *The bioethics of reproductive technologies: Impacts and implications for Latinas in Chicana critical issues.* Berkeley: Third Woman Press.

Fort, D. C. (1997). Feminism's lessons for women in science. *Journal of College Science Teaching, 27*(1), 53.

Foss-Fridlizius, R. (1990). Relativism och realism i feministisk vetenskapsfilosofi [Relativism and realism in a feminist philosophy of science]. *Kvinnovetenskaplig Tidskrift, 11*(3), 54–64.

Freedman, W. (1991). *Legal issues in biotechnology and human reproduction: Artificial conception and modern genetics.* New York: Quorum Books.

Furst, L. R. (Ed.). (1997). *Women healers and physicians: Climbing a long hill.* Lexington: University Press of Kentucky.

The future role of women in science and the world. (1980, January). *Chemist, 57*(1), 3–18.

Gaard, G. (1995). Ecofeminism and wilderness. *Environmental Ethics, 19*(1), 5.

Gaard, G. (1997, Winter). Toward a queer ecofeminism. *Hypatia, 12*(1), 114–137.

Gates, B. T., & Shteir, A. B. (1997). Natural eloquence: Women reinscribe science. *Isis, 88*(3), 587.

Gay, H. (1993). Saving the phenomena and saving conventions: A contribution to the debate over feminist epistemology. *Canadian Woman Studies/Les Cahiers de la Femme, 13*(2), 37–42.

Giese, P. A. (1992, Spring). Women in science: 5000 years of obstacles and achievements. *Appraisal: Science Books for Young People, 25*(2), 1–20.

Gimenez, M. E. (1991, September). The mode of reproduction in transition: A Marxist-feminist analysis of the effects of reproductive technologies. *Gender & Society, 5*(3), 334–350.

Ginsburg, F., & Rapp R. (1991). The politics of reproduction. *Annual Review of Anthropology, 20*, 311–343.

Ginsburg, F., & Rapp, R. (1995). *Conceiving the new world order: The global politics of reproduction.* Berkeley: University of California Press.

Glenn, B. P. (1996). The role of mentors for women in animal science: Perspectives from government. *Journal of Animal Science, 74*(11), 2855.

Goldberg, S. (1991, November 18). Feminism against science. (Feminism in everything from anthropology to physics). *National Review, 43*(21), 30–33.

Gomez, A., & Meacham, D. (1997). Bioethics and biotechnology: Marking the boundaries in a brave new world. *Women in Action, 97*(3), 74–77.

Goodman, M., & Goodman, L. E. (1981, September/October). Is there a feminist biology? *International Journal of Women's Studies, 4*(4), 393–413.

Gorham, G. (1995, Summer). The concept of truth in feminist sciences. *Hypatia, 10*(3), 99–116.

Gornick, V. (1995, March). Women in science. *Literary Cavalcade, 47*(6), 7.

Gottfried, H., & Esterberg, K. (1997). Feminism and social change: Bridging theory and practice. *Sociological Inquiry, 67*(2), 260–261.

Gottlieb, R. S. (1994, Summer). Ethics and trauma: Levinas, feminism, and deep ecology. *Cross Currents, 44*(2), 222.

Grady, M. M. (1995, July). Nobel prize women in science by S. Bertsch Mcgrayne. *Meteoritics, 30*(4), 472.

Grasselli, J. G., & Garrell, R.L. (1990, November). Women in science: A blueprint for progress. *Spectroscopy International, 2*(6), 16.

Green, K. (1994, Summer). Freud, Wollstonecraft, and ecofeminism. *Environmental Ethics, 16*(2), 117–134.

Green, K., & Bigelow, J. (1998).Does science persecute women? The case of the 16th–17th century witch-hunts. *Philosophy: The Journal of The British Institute of Philosophical Studies, 73*(284), 195.

Grint, K., & Gill, R. (1995). *The gender–technology relation: Contemporary theory and research.* Bristol, PA: Taylor & Francis.

Grint, K., & Woolgar, S. (1995). On some failures of nerve in constructivist and feminist analyses of technology. *Science, Technology, & Human Values, 20*(3), 286–330.

Gupta, A. (1997). Opportunities for women in science—The csir (extra mural research) experience. *Current Science, 72*(8), 549.

Gurer, D. W. (1995, January). Pioneering women in computer science. *Communications of the ACM, 38*(1), 45.

Haack, S. (1992). Science 'from a feminist perspective.' *Philosophy, 67*(259), 5–18.

Haberfeld, Y., & Shenhav, Y. (1990, October). Women and blacks closing the gap? Salary discrimination in American science in the 1970s and 1980s. *Industrial & Labor Relations Review, 44*(1), 68.

Hager, L. D. (Ed.). (1997). *Women in human evolution.* London & New York: Routledge.

Halberstam, J. (1991, Fall). Automating gender—Postmodern feminism in the age of the intelligent machine. *Feminist Studies, 17*, 439–460.

Hallen, P., Mies, M., & Shiva, V. (1995). Ecofeminism. *Women's Studies International Forum, 18*(3), 375.

Hallman, D. G. (1994). *Ecotheology: Voices from south and north.* Geneva, Switzerland: WCC Publications; Maryknoll, NY: Orbis Books.

Halpin, Z. (1989). Scientific objectivity and the concept of "the other." *Women's Studies International Forum, 12*(3), 285–294.

Hamrell, S., & Nordberg, O. (Eds.). (1993). *Women, ecology and health: Rebuilding connections.* Uppsala: Dag Hammarskjold Foundation.

A hand up: Women mentoring women in science. (1993, December 13). *Chemical and Engineering News, 71*(50), 49.

Hanson, S. L. (1996). *Lost talent: Women in the sciences.* Philadelphia: Temple University Press.

Haraway, D. (1987, Fall). Manifesto for cyborgs: Science, technology and socialist feminism in the 1980's. *Australian Feminist Studies,* no. 4, 1–42.

Haraway, D. (1989). Monkeys, aliens, and women: Love, science, and politics at the intersection of feminist theory and colonial discourse. *Women's Studies International Forum, 12*(3), 295–312.

Haraway, D. (1989). *Primate visions: Gender, race, and nature in the world of modern science.* New York: Routledge.

Haraway, D. (1991). *Simians, cyborgs, and women: The reinvention of nature.* New York: Routledge.

Haraway, D. (1994). A game of cat's cradle: Science studies, feminist theory, cultural studies. *Configurations: A Journal of Literature, Science, and Technology, 2*(1), 59.

Haraway, D. (1997). *Modest-witness@second-millennium.femaleman-meets-oncomouse: Feminism and technoscience.* New York: Routledge.

Harding, S. (1986). *The science question in feminism.* Ithaca, NY: Cornell University Press.

Harding, S. (1989). How the women's movement benefits science: Two views. *Women's Studies International Forum, 12*(3), 271–283.

Harding, S. (1989). Women as creators of knowledge: New environments. *American Behavioral Scientist, 32*(6), 700–707.

Harding, S. (1990). Feminism and theories of scientific knowledge. *Women: A Cultural Review, 1*(1), 87–98.

Harding, S. (1991). *Whose science? Whose knowledge?* Ithaca, NY: Cornell University Press.

Harding, S. (Ed.). (1993). *The "racial" economy of science: Toward a democratic future.* Bloomington: Indiana University Press.

Harding, S. (1993, Spring). II [Comment on Anne Fausto-Sterling's "Building two-way streets"]. *NWSA Journal, 5*(1), 49–55.

Harding, S. (1998). *Is science multicultural? Postcolonialisms, feminisms, and epistemologies.* Bloomington: Indiana University Press.

Harding, S. (1998, Summer). Gender, development, and post-enlightenment philosophies of science. [Special issue: Border crossings: Multicultural and postcolonial feminist challenges to philosophy, part 2]. *Hypatia, 13*(3), 146–167.

Harding, S., & Hintikka, M. B. (Eds.). (1983). *Discovering reality: Feminist perspectives on epistemology, metaphysics, methodology, and philosophy of science.* Dordrecht, Holland & Hingham, MA: D. Reidel.

Harding, S., & O'Barr, J. F. (Eds.). (1987). *Sex and scientific inquiry.* Chicago: University of Chicago Press.

Harris, J. (1992). *Wonderwoman and superman: The ethics of human biotechnology.* New York: Oxford University Press.

Hartouni, V. (1997). *Cultural conceptions: On reproductive technologies and the remaking of life.* Minneapolis: University of Minnesota Press.

Hawkins, R. Z. (1998, Winter). Ecofeminism and nonhumans: Continuity, difference, dualism, and domination. *Hypatia, 13*(1), 158–197.

Healy, B. (1992, March 13). Women in science: From panes to ceilings. *Science, 255* (5050), 1333–1334.

Heij, E. (1996). Women in science careers: Personal examples of some general factors. *Chemistry in Australia, 63*(5), 239.

Heller, R. S., & Martin, C. D. (1994, February). Attracting young minority women to engineering and science: Necessary characteristics for exemplary programs. *IEEE Transactions on Education, 37*(1), 8–12.

Helping hand for women. (1993, November 15). *The Scientist, 7*(22), 1.

Henderson, K. A. (1997). Ecofeminism and experiential education. *Journal of Experiential Education, 20*(3), 130.

Henwood, F. (1996). WISE choices? Understanding occupational decision-making in a climate of equal opportunities for women in science and technology. *Gender and Education, 8*(2), 199.

Herzenberg, C. L., & Howes, R. H. (1993, November). Women of the Manhattan Project. *Technology Review, 96*(8), 32–42.

Hicks, K. M. (1994). *Misdiagnosis: Woman as a disease.* Allentown, PA: People's Medical Society.

Higginbotham, E. (1997, Spring–Summer). Designing an inclusive curriculum: Bringing all women into the core. *Women's Studies Quarterly, 25*(1–2), 237–253.

Holloway, M. (1993, November). A lab of her own. *Scientific American, 269*(5), 94.

Holmes, H. B. (Ed.). (1992). *Issues in—Reproductive technology I: An anthology.* New York: Garland.

Holmes, H. B., & Purdy, L. M. (1992). *Feminist perspectives in medical ethics.* Bloomington: Indiana University Press.

Horn, D. G. (1994). *Social bodies: Science, reproduction, and Italian modernity.* Princeton, NJ: Princeton University Press.

Howell, K. (1993, June). The experience of women in undergraduate computer science: What does research say? *SIGCSE Bulletin, 25*(2), 1–8.

Howell, N. R. (1997, June). Ecofeminism: What one needs to know. *Zygon, 32*(2), 231–242.

Hoyrup, E. (1987). *Women of science, technology, and medicine: A bibliography.* Roskilde, Denmark: Roskilde University Library.

Hoyrup, E. (1989, June). Women of science, technology, and medicine: A bibliography. *Resources for Feminist Research, 18*(2), 82–83.

Hubbard, R. (1979). Reflections on the story of the double helix. *Women's Studies International Quarterly, 2*(3), 261–273.

Hubbard, R. (1984). "Fetal rights" and the new eugenics. *Science for the People, 16*(2), 7–9, 27–29.

Hubbard, R. (1988, Spring). Science, facts, and feminism. *Hypatia, 3*(1), 5–17.

Hubbard, R. (1990). *The politics of women's biology.* New Brunswick, NJ: Rutgers University Press.

Hubbard, R. (1993, Spring). I [Comment on Anne Fausto-Sterling's "Building two-way streets"]. *NWSA Journal, 5*(1), 45–48.

Hubbard, R. (1993, Winter). Of genies and bottles: Technology, values, and choices. *Canadian Woman Studies/Les Cahiers de la Femme, 13*(2), 82–84.

Hubbard, R. (1995). *Profitable promises: Essays on women, science, and health.* Monroe, ME: Common Courage Press.

Hubbard, R., & Berman, R. (1997). Profitable promises: Essays on women, science and health. *Science & Society, 61*(3), 423.

Hubbard, R., Henifin, M. S., & Fried, B. (1982). *Biological woman—The convenient myth: A collection of feminist essays and a bibliography.* Cambridge, MA: Schenkman.

Hubbard, R., & Wald, E. (1993). *Exploding the gene myth.* Boston: Beacon Press.

Hughes, D. M. (1991, August). Transforming science and technology: Has the elephant yet flicked its trunk? *NWSA Journal, 3*, 382–401.

The human genome: Ethical, political and social implications. (1997, April–June). *Women's Health Journal*, no. 2, 46–48.

Hunter, L., & Hutton, S. (Eds.). (1997). *Women, science and medicine 1500–1700: Mothers and sisters of the Royal Society.* Thrupp, Stroud, Gloucestershire: Sutton.

Hurtado, A. (1998, Spring). 'Sitios y lenguas': Chicanas theorize feminisms. [Special issue: Border crossings: Multicultural and postcolonial feminist challenges to philosophy, part 1]. *Hypatia, 13*(2), 134–161.

Hynes, P. (1989). *The recurring silent spring.* New York: Pergamon Press.

Hynes, P. H. (Ed.). (1991). *Reconstructing Babylon: Essays on women and technology.* Bloomington: Indiana University Press.

Imber, B., & Tuana, N. (1988, Spring). Feminist perspectives on science. *Hypatia, 3*(1), 139–144.

Improving opportunities for women in science. (1992, August). *ASM News, 58*(8), 410.

In my view . . . deer hunters at bay; women in science, women in Europe; what's in a title? (1997). *Biologist: Journal of the Institute of Biology, 44*(3), 337.

Increasing the participation of women in science. (1990, March 5). *The Scientist, 4*(5), 17.

Irvine, J., & Martin, B. R. (1982). Women in science—The astronomical brain drain. *Women's Studies International Forum, 5*(1), 41–68.

Jackson, A. (1990, January 5). Encouraging women in math and science. *Notices of the American Mathematical Society, 37*(1), 5–6.

Jackson, C. (1995, March–April). Radical environmental myths: A gender perspective. *New Left Review*, no. 210, 124–142.

Jacobus, M., Keller, E. F., & Shuttleworth, S. (Eds.). (1990). *Body/politics: Women and the discourses of science.* New York: Routledge.

Jahren, N., & Ginzberg, R. (1990, Spring). Comments on Ruth Ginzberg's paper "Uncovering gynocentric science" with reply. *Hypatia, 5*(1), 171–180.

Jaggar, A. M. (1998, Spring). Globalizing feminist ethics. [Special issue: Border crossings: Multicultural and postcolonial feminist challenges to philosophy, part 1]. *Hypatia, 13*(2), 7–31.

Jaggar, A. M., & Bordo, S. (Eds.). (1989). *Gender/body/knowledge: Feminist reconstructions of being and knowing.* New Brunswick, NJ: Rutgers University Press.

Jezer, R. (1991). Congressional actions re women in science and mathematics. *Bulletin of Science, Technology & Society, 11*(3), 134–137.

John, M. E. (1996). *Discrepant dislocations: Feminism, theory and postcolonial histories.* Berkeley: University of California Press.

Jordanova, L. J. (1989). *Sexual visions: Images of gender in science and medicine between the eighteenth and twentieth centuries.* Madison: University of Wisconsin Press.

Kaminsky, A. (1994, Spring). Gender, race, raza. *Feminist Studies, 20*(1), 7–32.

Kaplan, L. J., & Tong, R. (1994). *Controlling our reproductive destiny: A technological and philosophical perspective.* Cambridge, MA: MIT Press.

Keeble, S. (1994). *Infertility, feminism and the new technologies.* London: Fabian Society.

Keller, E. F. (1980). Feminist critique of science: A forward or backward move? *Fundamenta Scientiae, 1*(3/4), 341–349.

Keller, E. F. (1990, October 15). Equal opportunities. *The Scientist, 4*(20), 15.

Keller, E. F. (1992). *Secrets of life, secrets of death: Essays on science and culture.* New York: Routledge.

Keller, E. F., & Longino, H. E. (Eds.). (1995). *Feminism and science.* New York: Oxford University Press.

Kelly, F. (Ed.). (1993). *On the edge of discovery: Australian women in science.* Melbourne: Text Publishing Co.

Kerr, E. A. (1997, January–February). Toward a feminist natural science: Linking theory and practice. *Women's Studies International Forum, 21*(1), 95–109.

Ketchum, S. A. (1989, Fall). Selling babies and selling bodies. *Hypatia, 4*(3), 116–127.

Kevles, D. J., & Hood, L. (Eds.). (1993). *The code of codes: Scientific and social issues in the Human Genome Project.* Cambridge, MA: Harvard University Press.

Khazanet, V. (1996).Women in civil engineering and science: It's time for recognition and promotion. *Journal of Professional Issues in Engineering Education and Practice, 122*(2), 65.

Kim, S. H. (1995, Winter). Perspectives on women in science and medicine. *Yale Scientific, 69*(1), 5.

Kimball, M. (1981, September/October). Women and science: A critique of biological theories. *International Journal of Women's Studies, 4*(4), 318–338.

King, Y. (1995, Fall). Engendering a peaceful planet: Ecology, economy, and ecofeminism in contemporary context. *Women's Studies Quarterly, 23*(3–4), 15.

Kirk, (1997). Ecofeminism and environmental justice: Bridges across gender, race, and class. *Frontiers, 18*(2), 2.

Klawiter, M. (1990, Fall). Using Arendt and Heidegger to consider feminist thinking on women and reproductive/infertility technologies. *Hypatia, 5*(3), 65–90.

Klein, R. D., & Minden, S. (1981). Feminists in science speak up: Alice through the microscope—The latest in a series of books on women and science. *Women's Studies International Quarterly, 4*(2), 241–252.

Koch, J. (1998). Lab coats and little girls: The science experiences of women majoring in biology and education at a private university. *Contributions in Women's Studies, 164,* 175.

Koertge, N. (1994). Do feminists alienate women from the sciences? *The Education Digest, 60*(4), 49–52.

Koertge, N. (1995, March–April). How feminism is now alienating women from science. *Skeptical Inquirer, 19*(2), 42–43.

Kollek, R. (1990). Limits of experimental knowledge: A feminist perspective on the ecological risks of genetic engineering. *Reproductive & Genetic Engineering, 3*(2), 125–136.

Komesaroff, P. A. (1995). *Troubled bodies: Critical perspectives on postmodernism, medical ethics, and the body.* Durham, NC: Duke University Press.

Kourany, J. A. (Ed.). (1998). *Philosophy in a feminist voice: Critiques and reconstructions.* Princeton, NJ: Princeton University Press.

Kramarae, C., & Spender, D. (1992). *The knowledge explosion: Generations of feminist scholarship.* New York: Teachers College Press.

Kremer, K. B., Mullins, G. W., & Roth, R. E. (1991, Winter). Women in science and environmental education: Need for an agenda. *Journal of Environmental Education, 22*(2), 4–6.

Krishnaraj, M. (1980, Spring). The status of women in science in India. *Journal of Higher Education, 5,* 381–393.

Lamas, M. (1997, April–June). Bioethics: Social process and changing values. *Women's Health Journal, 2/97,* 35–37.

Landau, I. (1996, January). How androcentric is western philosophy? *Philosophical Quarterly, 46*(182), 48–59.

Lange, L. (1998, Summer). Burnt offerings to rationality: A feminist reading of the construction of indigenous peoples in Enrique Dussel's theory of modernity. [Special issue: Border crossings: Multicultural and postcolonial feminist challenges to philosophy, part 2]. *Hypatia, 13*(3), 132–145.

Lanzinger, I. (1993, Winter). Toward feminist science teaching. *Canadian Woman Studies/Les Cahiers de la Femme, 13*(2), 95–99.

Lauritzen, P. (1990, March–April). What price parenthood? *The Hastings Center Report, 20*(2), 38–46.

Lauritzen, P. (1993). *Pursuing parenthood: Ethical issues in assisted reproduction.* Bloomington: Indiana University Press.

Lay, S. (1994). Ecofeminism by Maria Mies & Vandana Shiva. *Race & Class, 36*(1), 105.

Lederman, M. (1993). Structuring feminist science. *Women's Studies International Forum, 16*(6), 605–613.

Lenfant, C. (1993, October). Women in biomedical science: Through the looking glass. *Circulation, 88*(4), 1409.

Leslie, L. L., Mcclure, G. T., & Oaxaca, R. L. (1998). Women and minorities in science and engineering: A life sequence analysis. *Journal of Higher Education, 69*(3), 239.

Liesen, L. T. (1995, August). Feminism and the politics of reproductive strategies. *Politics and the Life Sciences,* pp. 145–162.

Link, C. (1998). Women in science—Attracting more women and minorities to the sciences. *Journal of College Science Teaching, 28*(1), 26.

Lippman, A. (1995). "Never too late": Biotechnology, women and reproduction. *McGill Law Journal/Revue de Droit de McGill, 40*(4), 875.

Lips, H. M., & Temple, L. (1990, February). Majoring in computer science: Causal models for women and men. *Research in Higher Education, 31*(1), 99.

Lock, M., & Kaufert, P. A. (Eds.). (1998). *Pragmatic women and body politics.* New York: Cambridge University Press.

Longino, H. (1989). Feminist critiques of rationality: Critiques of science or philosophy of science? *Women's Studies International Forum, 12*(3), 261–269.

Longino, H. (1990). *Science as social knowledge.* Princeton, NJ: Princeton University Press.

Longino, H. E. (1992, September–December). Knowledge, bodies, and values: Reproductive technologies and their scientific context. *Inquiry (An Interdisciplinary Journal of Philosophy), 35*(3–4), 323–340.

Longino, H. E. (1993, Autumn). Feminist standpoint theory and the problems of knowledge. *Signs, 19*(1), 201–212.

Lootens, T. (1984, October). "Feminist science": A meaningful concept? *off our backs, 14,* 13.

Lorber, J. (1989, Fall). Choice, gift, or patriarchal bargain? Women's consent to in vitro fertilization in male infertility. *Hypatia, 4*(3), 23–36.

Lorber, J. (1993). Believing is seeing: Biology as ideology. *Gender & Society, 7*(4), 568–581.

Lorber, J. (1997). *Gender and the social construction of illness.* Thousand Oaks, CA: Sage.

Lorrigan, G. (1995). Science—Whose knowledge? *Broadsheet: New Zealand Feminist Magazine,* no. 205, 24–25.

Lowe, M. (1993, Winter). To understand the world in order to change it [Margaret Benston]. *Canadian Woman Studies/Les Cahiers de la Femme, 13*(2), 6–11.

Lowe, M., & Hubbard, R. (1983). *Woman's nature: Rationalizations of inequality.* New York: Pergamon Press.

Lublin, N. (1998). *Pandora's box: Feminism confronts reproductive technology.* Lanham, MD: Rowman & Littlefield.

Luria, Z. (1988, March). Science, biology, and gender. *Psychology of Women Quarterly, 12,* 123–125.

Lykke, N., & Braidotti, R. (1996). *Between monsters, goddesses, and cyborgs: Feminist confrontations with science, medicine, and cyberspace.* London: Zed Books.

Lyon, J. (1991, Fall). Transforming manifestoes: A second-wave problematic. (Feminist manifestoes). *Yale Journal of Criticism, 5*(1), 101–128.

MacColl, S. (1990, Summer). Universality and difference: O'Keeffe and McClintock. (Georgia O'Keeffe, Barbara McClintock). *Hypatia, 5*(2), 147–157.

Macdonald, C. (1994). Women in science. *The Genetic Engineer & Biotechnologist, 14*(4), 219.

Makhubu L. P. (1994). The role of women in relation to the environment. In F. Graham-Smith (Ed.), *Population—The complex reality* (Report of the Population

Summit of the World's Scientific Academies; pp. 199–209). London: Royal Society.

Malm, H. M. (1989, Fall). Commodification or compensation: A reply to Ketchum. (Sara Ann Ketchum). *Hypatia, 4*(3), 128.

Mandell, N. (1995). *Feminist issues: Race, class, and sexuality.* Scarborough, ON: Prentice-Hall.

Manning, K. R. (1991, November). The complexion of science. *Technology Review, 94*(8), 60.

Mansour, D., Elabass, M. A., & Abdelmageed, A. The role of Sudanese women in the field of science and technology: Obstacles and future prospects. *Ahfad Journal: Women and Change, 13*(1), 38–46.

Manthorpe, C. (1985, March 7). Feminists look at science. *New Scientist, 105,* 29–31.

Mark, H. F. L. (1995). Commentary—The concern for the plight of women in science has received much attention but little commitment on the part of government and academia. *The Scientist, 9*(18), 13.

Marsden, C., & Omery, A. (1992). Women, science, and a women's science. *Women's Studies, 21*(4), 479–489.

Martin, E. (1987). *The woman in the body.* Boston: Beacon Press.

Mason, J. (1992). Women in science: Breaking out of the circle. *Notes and Records of the Royal Society of London, 46,* 177–182.

Masters, R. D. (1995, August). From inclusive fitness to neuroscience: Proximate mechanisms, feminism, and the politics of gender. *Politics and the Life Sciences,* pp. 180–183.

McCallum, P. (1995, January). Introductory notes: Postcolonialism and its discontents. *ARIEL, 26*(1), 7–22.

McCaughey, M. (1993). Redirecting feminist critiques of science. *Hypatia, 8*(4), 72–84.

McConnell, R. A. (1995). *Far out in the new age: The subversion of science by cultural communism: A compendium of current social controversy.* Pittsburgh: R. A. McConnell.

McCormick, N., & McCormick, J. (1991, September). Not for men only: Why so few women major in computer science. *College Student Journal, 25*(3), 345–350.

McDaniel, S. A. (1996, Winter). Toward a synthesis of feminist and demographic perspectives on fertility. *Sociological Quarterly, 37*(1), 83–104.

McGowan, T. D. (1992). The metaphysical science of Aristotle's generation of animals and its feminist critics. *Review of Metaphysics, 46*(2), 307–342.

McIlwee, J. S., & Robinson, J. G. (1992). *Women in engineering: Gender, power, and workplace culture.* Albany: State University of New York Press.

McIntosh, A. (1996). The emperor has no clothes . . . let us paint our loinclothes rainbow: A classical and feminist critique of contemporary science policy. *Environmental Values, 5*(1), 3–30.

McKenna, E., & Warren, K. J. (1998). Ecofeminism: Women, culture, nature. *Teaching Philosophy, 21*(2), 189.

McLennan, G. (1995, August). Feminism, epistemology and postmodernism: Reflections on current ambivalence. *Sociology, 29*(3), 391–410.

McMahon, M. (1997). From the ground up: Ecofeminism and ecological economics.

Ecological Economics: The Journal of the International Society for Ecological Economics, 20(2), 163.

McWilliam, E., & Taylor, P. G. (1996). *Pedagogy, technology, and the body.* New York: Peter Lang.

Mendus, S. (1996, January). How androcentric is western philosophy? A reply. (Response to I. Landau in same issue, pp. 48–59). *Philosophical Quarterly, 46*(182), 60–65.

Mentoring maneuvers. (1993, July 26). *The Scientist, 7*(15), 1.

Menzies, H. (1987, May–June). In his image: Science and technology as ideology. *This Magazine, 21,* 31–34.

Menzies, H. (1991, Fall). Science through her looking glass. *Women's Education/ Education des Femmes, 9*(2), 31–34.

Merchant, C. (1989). *Ecological revolutions: Nature, gender, and science in New England.* Chapel Hill: University of North Carolina Press.

Merchant, C. (1990). *The death of nature: Women, ecology, and the scientific revolution.* San Francisco: Harper & Row.

Merchant, C. (1992, Summer). Perspectives on ecofeminism: Viewpoint. *Environmental Action Magazine, 24*(2), 18.

Merchant, J. (1996). Confronting the consequences of medical technology: Policy frontiers in the United States and France. In M. Githens & D. M. Stetson (Eds.), *Abortion politics: Public policy in cross-cultural perspective* (pp. 189–209). New York: Routledge.

Meyer, C. L. (1997). *The wandering uterus: Politics and the reproductive rights of women.* New York: New York University Press.

Michie, H., & Cahn, N. R. (1997). *Confinements: Fertility and infertility in contemporary culture.* New Brunswick, NJ: Rutgers University Press.

Mies, M. (1988). From the individual to the individual: In the supermarket of "reproductive alternatives." *Reproductive and Genetic Engineering, 1*(3), 225–237.

Mies, M. (1990). Women's studies—Science, violence, and responsibility. *Women's Studies International Forum, 13*(5), 433–441.

Mies, M., & Shiva, V. (1993). *Ecofeminism.* Atlantic Highlands, NJ: Zed Books.

Mies, M., & Shiva, V. (1997). Ecofeminism. *Women & Politics, 18*(1), 104.

Mies, M., Shiva, V., & Gaard, G. (1996). Ecofeminism and Val Plumwood: Feminism and the mastery of nature. *Environmental Ethics, 18*(1), 93.

Mongia, P. (Ed.). (1996). *Contemporary postcolonial theory: A reader.* New York: St. Martin's Press.

Morgall, J. M. (1991). *Developing technology assessment: A critical feminist approach.* Lund, Sweden: J. M. Morgall.

Morgan, C. S. (1992, December). College students' perceptions of barriers to women in science and engineering. *Youth & Society, 24*(2), 228.

Morgan, R. (1982, December). Feminist notes: A quantum leap in feminist theory. *Ms. Magazine, 11*(6), 101–106.

Morton, S., Okruhlik, K., Thielen-Wilson, L., & Wylie, A. (1989). Bibliography on feminism and science. Feminist critiques of science: The epistemological and methodological literature. *Women's Studies International Forum, 12*(3), 379–388.

Muller, C. B. (1992, Fall). The women in science project at Dartmouth. *Initiatives,* *55*(3), 39–48.

Muller, C., & Pavone, M. L. (1997). Retaining undergraduate women in science, math, and engineering: A model program. *Proceedings of the Conference on Frontiers in Education, 1,* 120.

Munoz, E. A., & Weaver, F. S. (1997). "Out of place": Ecuadorian women in science and engineering programs. *Latin American Perspectives, 24*(4), 81.

Mura, R. (1991). *Searching for subjectivity in the world of the sciences: Feminist viewpoints.* Ottawa: Canadian Research Institute for the Advancement of Women / Institut Canadien de Recherches sur les Femmes.

Mura, R. (1992–1993, Fall–Summer). Feminist critiques of science: A menace to women and science? An analysis of two reactions by mathematicians. [Les critiques fiministes de la science: Une menace aux femmes et la science? analyse de deux riactions du milieu mathimatique.] *Atlantis: A Women's Studies Journal/Revue d'Etudes sur les Femmes, 18*(1–2), 3–24.

Murphy, J. S. (1989, Fall). Is pregnancy necessary? Feminist concerns about ectogenesis. *Hypatia, 4*(3), 66–84.

Mutima, N. (1995). Women in science and technology (WIST)—Workshop on professional development and project formulation. *Discovery and Innovation, 7*(2), 104.

Nadeau, R. (1996). *S/he brain: Science, sexual politics, and the myths of feminism.* Westport, CT: Praeger.

Narayan, U. (1995, Spring). Colonialism and its others: Considerations on rights and care discourses. *Hypatia, 10*(2), 133–140.

Narayan, U. (1998, Spring). Essence of culture and a sense of history: A feminist critique of cultural essentialism. [Special issue: Border crossings: Multicultural and postcolonial feminist challenges to philosophy, part 1]. *Hypatia, 13*(2), 86–106.

Neeley, K. A. (1992, December). Woman as mediatrix: Women as writers on science and technology in the eighteenth and nineteenth centuries. *IEEE Transactions on Professional Communication, 35*(4), 208–216.

Nelson, H. L., & Nelson, J. L. (1989, Fall). Cutting motherhood in two: Some suspicions concerning surrogacy. *Hypatia, 4*(3), 85–94.

Nelson, J. A. (1997). Feminism, ecology and the philosophy of economics. *Ecological Economics: The Journal of the International Society for Ecological Economics, 20*(2), 155.

Nelson, L. (1991). Feminist science criticism and critical thinking. *Transformations, 2*(1), 26–35.

Nelson, L. (1995). A feminist naturalized philosophy of science. *Synthese, 104*(3), 399–422.

Nelson, L. H., & Nelson, J. (Eds.). (1996). *Feminism, science, and the philosophy of science.* Dordrecht & Boston: Kluwer.

Nicholson, L. (1990). *Feminism/postmodernism.* New York: Routledge.

Nielsen, F. (1995, August). Feminism and selfish genes. *Politics and the Life Sciences,* pp. 182–184.

Noble, D. F. (1992). *A world without women: The Christian clerical culture of western science*. New York: Knopf.

Nyoongah, J. L. (1996, October). The race for race: Feminist scholarship and the positionality impasse. (Focus on Asia and Australia). *Hecate, 22*(2), 130–139.

Oakley, A. (1993). *Essays on women, medicine and health*. Edinburgh: Edinburgh University Press.

Oakley, A. (1998, March–April). Science, gender, and women's liberation: An argument against postmodernism. *Women's Studies International Forum, 21*(2), 133–146.

Oaks, A. B. (1992). Empowering women in mathematics. *Initiatives, 55*(2), 31–38.

O'Bannon, B. (1994).The Narmada River Project: Toward a feminist model of women in development. *Policy Sciences, 27*(2–3), 247.

O'Brien, M. (1981). *The politics of reproduction*. Boston: Routledge & Kegan Paul.

Odeh, L. A. (1993, Spring). Post-colonial feminism and the veil: Thinking the difference. *Feminist Review*, no. 43, 26–37.

Offerman-Zuckerberg, J. (Ed.). (1989). *Gender in transition: A new frontier*. New York: Plenum Medical.

Ogilvie, M. B. (1996). *Women in science: An annotated bibliography*. New York: Garland.

Ogilvie, M. B., Meek, K. L., & Shearer, B. (1997). Women and science: An annotated bibliography. *Isis, 88*(2), 382.

Okin, S. M. (1998, Spring). Feminism, women's human rights, and cultural differences. [Special issue: Border crossings: Multicultural and postcolonial feminist challenges to philosophy, part 1]. *Hypatia, 13*(2), 32–52.

Opie, A. (1992, Spring). Qualitative research, appropriation of the "other" and empowerment. *Feminist Review*, no. 40, 52–69.

Osborn, M. (1994, March 11). Status and prospects of women in science in Europe. *Science, 263*(11), 1389.

O'Sullivan, S. (1987). *Women's health: A spare rib reader*. New York: Pandora Press.

Overall, C. (Ed.). (1989). *The future of human reproduction*. Toronto: Women's Press.

Participation of women in science and technology industry. (1995). *Official Journal of the European Communities: Information and Notices, 38*(209), 45.

Pathways for women in science. (1994, March 21). *The Scientist, 8*(6), 11.

Patterson, R. M. (1989, Fall). Black women in the biological sciences. *Sage, 6*(2), 8–14.

Paul, D. B. (1995). *Controlling human heredity, 1865 to the present*. Atlantic Highlands, NJ: Humanities Press.

Penry, D. (1997). Women in science. *Journal of College Science Teaching, 26*(5), 360.

Petersen, K. A. (1997). *Intersections—Women on law, medicine, and technology*. Brookfield, VT: Ashgate/Dartmouth.

Pfafflin, S. M. (1984, October). Women, science and technology. *American Psychologist, 39*, 1183–1186.

Phillips, P. (1990). *The scientific lady: A social history of women's scientific interests, 1520–1918*. New York: St. Martin's Press.

Phillips, P. S., & McKay, R. (1994). Women in science: A brief history within chemistry. *School Science Review, 76*(274), 132.

Pinnick, C. L. (1994). Feminist epistemology: Implications for philosophy of science. *Philosophy of Science, 61*(4), 646–657.

Plumwood, V. (1991, Spring). Nature, self, and gender: Feminism, environmental philosophy, and the critique of rationalism. *Hypatia, 6*(1), 3–27.

Plumwood, V. (1992, January). Beyond the dualistic assumptions of women, men and nature. *The Ecologist, 22*(1), 8–13.

Pois, A. M. (1995, October 1). Foreshadowings. *Peace and Change, 20*(4), 439.

Posada, C. (1994). Interview with Carmen Posada: Let's develop a feminist bioethics. *Women in Action*, no. 2/3, 35–36.

Preston, A. E. (1994, December). Why have all the women gone? A study of exit of women from the science and engineering professions. *American Economic Review, 84*(5), 1446.

Prey, J., & Baldwin, D. (1997). Measuring factors affecting women in undergraduate computer science. *SIGCSE Bulletin, 29*(1), 395.

Professional *forum*—What's the to do with women in science and engineering? (1995, October 12). *Chemical Engineer*, no. 597, 46.

Puka, B. (1991, Summer). The science of caring. (A response to S. Elise Peeples's comment, "Her terrain is outside his 'domain.'"). *Hypatia, 6*(2), 200–210.

Purdy, L. M. (1996). *Reproducing persons: Issues in feminist bioethics*. Ithaca, NY: Cornell University Press.

Purdy, L. M. (1996, October). What can progress in reproductive technology mean for women? *The Journal of Medicine and Philosophy, 21*(5), 499–514.

Ramazanoglu, C. (1992, May). On feminist methodology: Male reason versus female empowerment (response to article by M. Hammersley in this issue). *Sociology, 26*(2), 207–212.

Rapp, R. (1987). Moral pioneers: Women, men and fetuses on a frontier of reproductive technology. *Women & Health, 13*(1/2), 101–116.

Rapuro, O. (1997, November 11). Kenyan women are defying long held myths about women's performance in science studies, and are becoming increasingly aware of their scientific capabilities and the role they can play in developing in the country. Available from Interpress Service.

Ratcliff, K. S. (Ed.). (1989). *Healing technology: Feminist perspectives*. Ann Arbor: University of Michigan Press.

Ray, S. (1992, Spring). Shifting subjects shifting ground: The names and spaces of the post-colonial. *Hypatia, 7*(2), 188–201.

Rayman, P., & Brett, B. (1993). *Pathways for women in the sciences*. Wellesley, MA: Wellesley College Center for Research on Women.

Rayman, P., & Brett, B. (1995). Women science majors: What makes a difference in persistence after graduation? *Journal of Higher Education, 66*(4), 388.

Raymond, J. G. (1989). Reproductive technologies, radical feminism, and socialist liberalism. *Reproductive & Genetic Engineering, 2*(2), 133–142.

Raymond, J. G. (1993). *Women as wombs: Reproductive technologies and the battle over women's freedom*. San Francisco: Harper.

Reid, K. (1995, Spring). Women in physical science. *Science and Public Affairs*, no. 1, 4.

Report looks at retaining women in science and math. (1994, February 16). *Chronicle of Higher Education*, p. A41.

Riger, S. (1992, June). Epistemological debates, feminist voices: Science, social values, and the study of women. *American Psychologist, 47*(6), 730–740.

Roberts, H. (1981). *Women, health, and reproduction*. Boston: Routledge & Kegan Paul.

Rose, H. (1983, Autumn). Hand, brain, and heart: A feminist epistemology for the natural sciences. *Signs, 9*(1), 73–90.

Rose, H. (1989). Talking about science as a socialist-feminist. *Rethinking Marxism, 2*(3), 26–30.

Rose, H. (1994). *Love, power, and knowledge: Towards a feminist transformation of the sciences*. Bloomington: Indiana University Press.

Rose, H. (1994, May 13). A feminist science? *New Statesman & Society, 7*(302), 29.

Rosser, S. V. (1984, January/February). Call for feminist science. *International Journal of Women's Studies, 7*(1), 3–9.

Rosser, S. V. (1986). *Teaching science and health from a feminist perspective: A practical guide*. New York: Pergamon Press.

Rosser, S. V. (1988). *Feminism within the science and health care professions: Overcoming resistance*. Elmsford, New York: Pergamon Press.

Rosser, S. V. (1988). Good science: Can it ever be gender free? *Women's Studies International Forum, 11*(1), 13–19.

Rosser, S. V. (1989). Re-visioning clinical research: Gender and the ethics of experimental design. *Hypatia, 4*(2), 125–139.

Rosser, S. V. (1989). Ruth Bleier: A passionate vision for feminism and science. *Women's Studies International Forum, 12*(3), 249–252.

Rosser, S. V. (1989). Teaching techniques to attract women to science: Applications of feminist theories and methodologies. *Women's Studies International Forum, 2*(3), 363–378.

Rosser, S. V. (1992). *Biology & feminism: A dynamic interaction*. New York: Twayne.

Rosser, S. V. (1992, September–December). Are there feminist methodologies appropriate for the natural sciences and do they make a difference? *Women's Studies International Forum, 15*(5–6), 535–550.

Rosser, S. V. (1993, Spring). IV [Comment on Anne Fausto-Sterling's "Building two-way streets"]. *NWSA Journal, 5*(1), 65–76.

Rosser, S. V. (1994). *Women's health—Missing from U.S. medicine*. Bloomington: Indiana University Press.

Rothman, B. K. (1982, July/August). How science is redefining parenthood. *Ms. Magazine, 11*(1/2), 154–156.

Rothman, B. K. (1985). The products of conception: The social context of reproductive choices. *Journal of Medical Ethics, 11*, 191.

Rothman, B. K. (1989). *Recreating motherhood: Ideology and technology in a patriarchal society*. New York: Norton.

Rothschild, J. (1983). *Machina ex dea: Feminist perspectives on technology*. New York: Teachers College Press.

Rothschild, J., & Frederick, F. (1993). *Technology and feminism*. Greenwich, CT: JAI Press.

Rouse, J. (1991, December). The politics of postmodern philosophy of science. *Philosophy of Science, 58*(4), 607–627.

Rowland, R. (1992). *Living laboratories: Women and reproductive technologies*. Bloomington: Indiana University Press.

Rowold, K. (Ed.). (1996). *Gender and science: Late nineteenth-century debates on the female mind and body*. Bristol: Thoemmes Press.

Rundblad, G. (1990). Feminism and the constructions of knowledge: Speculations on a subjective science. *Women and Language, 13*(1), 53–55.

Rutnam, R. (1991). IVF in Australia: Towards a feminist technology assessment. *Reproductive & Genetic Engineering, 4*(2), 143–154.

Ruzek, S. B. (1978). *The women's health movement: Feminist alternatives to medical control*. New York: Praeger.

Ryle, M., & Mellor, M. (1998). Feminism and ecology. *The Times Literary Supplement*, no. 4963, 28.

Safford, B. (1990, Spring). Comment on Zita's review of *The science question in feminism*. *Hypatia, 5*(1), 181.

Sakai, A. K., & Lane, M. J. (1996). Roundtable: National Science Foundation funding patterns of women and minorities in biology. *Bioscience, 46*(8), 621.

Salleh, A. (1992, Fall). The ecofeminism/deep ecology debate: A reply to patriarchal reason. *Environmental Ethics, 14*(3), 195–216.

Salleh, A. (1993, Fall). Class, race, and gender discourse in the ecofeminism/deep ecology debate. *Environmental Ethics, 15*(3), 225–244.

Salters, R. E. (1997). Pursuing the Ph.D. in the sciences and engineering: Trends and observations—Science and engineering doctoral education has changed because of shifts in university, industry, and government influences, and it must continue to change by attracting and encouraging women and underrepresented groups. *New Directions for Higher Education*, no. 99, 91.

Sandilands, C. (1997). Wild democracy: Ecofeminism, politics and the desire beyond. *Frontiers, 18*(2), 135.

Sandilands, C. (1997, Fall). Mother earth, the cyborg, and the queer: Ecofeminism and (more) questions of identity. *NWSA Journal, 9*(3), 18.

Saunders, J. (1991). *Non-human nature and feminism: Towards a green feminist theory*. Worcester, MA: Worcester College of Higher Education.

Sayers, J. (1987). Feminism and science—Reason and passion. *Women's Studies International Forum, 10*(2), 171–179.

Scharff, V. (1995, Summer). Are earth girls easy? Ecofeminism, women's history and environmental history. *Journal of Women's History, 7*(2), 164.

Schick, I. C. (1990, Summer). Representing Middle Eastern women: Feminism and colonial discourse. *Feminist Studies, 16*(2), 345.

Schiebinger, L. (1987). History and philosophy of women in science: A review essay. *Signs, 12*(2), 305–332.

Schiebinger, L. (1989). *The mind has no sex? Women in the origins of modern science.* Cambridge, MA: Harvard University Press.

Schiebinger, L. (1990). The anatomy of difference: Race and gender in eighteenth-century science. *Eighteenth-Century Studies, 23,* 387–406.

Schiebinger, L. (1993). *Nature's body: Gender in the making of modern science.* Boston: Beacon Press.

Schiebinger, L. (1999). *Has feminism changed science?* Cambridge, MA: Harvard University Press.

Schneiderman, J. S. (1997, Fall). The common interests of earth science, feminism, and environmental justice. *NWSA Journal, 9*(3), 124–137.

Schrijvers, J. (1995). Feminist science and research philosophy: History and general principles. In *Gender, reproductive health and population policies: Reports from the Manila Workshop, 7–10 April 1994* (pp. 35–61). Quezon City, Philippines: Health Action Information Network.

Schurrman, N. (1986, April). Prognosis grim for science. *Kinesis,* p. 19.

Schutte, O. (1998, Spring). Cultural alterity: Cross-cultural communication and feminist theory in north–south contexts. [Special issue: Border crossings: Multicultural and postcolonial feminist challenges to philosophy, part 1]. *Hypatia, 13*(2), 53–72.

Science and technology—Bias against women scientists. (1997). *The Economist, 343*(8018), 129.

Science and technology—Women in science. (1996). *The Economist, 339*(7971), 97.

Science insights: Women now earn almost a third of all Ph.Ds in chemistry, but they are still hard to find as speakers at symposia. (1997). *Chemical and Engineering News, 75*(30), 41.

Science insights: Women scientists and philosophers need to learn to communicate. (1997). *Chemical and Engineering News, 75*(17), 30.

The science of inclusion. (1991, September 16). *The Scientist, 5*(18), 1.

Science's next wave—Women in forum: It's never too late to return to science. (1997). *Science, 276*(5313), 837.

Scott, C. V. (1996). *Gender and development: Rethinking modernization and dependency theory.* Boulder, CO: Lynne Rienner.

Scragg, G., & Smith, J. (1998). A study of barriers to women in undergraduate computer science. *SIGCSE Bulletin, 30*(1), 82.

Scutt, J. A. (1990). *The baby machine: Reproductive technology and the commercialisation of motherhood.* London: Green Print.

Seager, J. (1993). *Earth follies: Coming to feminist terms with the global environmental crisis.* New York: Routledge.

Seidman, S. (1994). *The postmodern turn: New perspectives on social theory.* New York: Cambridge University Press.

Sessions, R. (1991, Spring). Deep ecology versus ecofeminism: Healthy differences or incompatible philosophies? *Hypatia, 6*(1), 90–107.

Seymour, E. (1995). The loss of women from science, mathematics, and engineering undergraduate majors: An explanatory account. *Science Education, 79*(4), 437.

Shearer, R. R., & Gaard, G. (1997). Ecofeminism, women, animals, nature. *Signs*, 22(2), 496.

Sheinin, R. (1984, Summer). Women in science: Issues and actions. *Canadian Woman Studies/Les Cahiers de la Femme*, 5(4), 70–77.

Sherwin, S. (1992). *No longer patient: Feminist ethics and health care*. Philadelphia: Temple University Press.

Shinn, J. (1993, April). Getting into science and technology. *Common Ground*, 12(2), 25.

Shiva, V. (1992, January). The seed and the earth: Women, ecology and biotechnology. *The Ecologist*, 22(1), 4–7.

Shiva, V. (Ed.). (1993). *Minding our lives: Women from the south and north reconnect ecology and health*. Philadelphia: New Society.

Shiva, V. (Ed.). (1994). *Close to home: Women reconnect ecology, health, and development worldwide*. Philadelphia: New Society.

Shiva, V. (1996, April/May/June). The planet is our household. *Women's Health Journal*, no. 2, 4–12.

Shiva, V. (1997, Spring). Economic globalization, ecological feminism, and sustainable development. *Canadian Woman Studies/Les Cahiers de la Femme*, 17(2), 22–27.

Shiva, V., & Moser, I. (Eds.). (1995). *Biopolitics: A feminist and ecological reader on biotechnology*. London: Zed Books.

Shteir, A. B., & Drayton, R. (1997). Cultivating women, cultivating science: Flora's daughters and botany in England, 1760–1860. *Isis*, 88(3), 546.

Siebers, T. (Ed.). (1994). *Heterotopia: Postmodern utopia and the body politic*. Ann Arbor: University of Michigan Press.

Sim, C. N. C., & Hensman, R. (1994). Science and technology: Friends or enemies of women? *Journal of Gender Studies*, 3(3), 277–287.

Simmons, P. (1992, January). The challenge of feminism. *The Ecologist*, 22(1), 2–3.

Slicer, D. (1995, Summer). Is there an ecofeminism–deep ecology "debate"? *Environmental Ethics*, 17(2), 151–170.

Sloat, B. F. (1992). Undergraduate women in the sciences: Removing barriers. *Initiatives*, 55(2), 5–10.

Slowly rising diversity in science. (1994, March 7). *The Scientist*, 8(5), 3.

Smith, J. (1980). Something old, something new, something borrowed, something due: Women and appropriate technology. Missoula, MT: Women and Technology Project.

Soble, A. (1994, October). Gender, objectivity, and realism. (Psychoanalytic account of science by Evelyn Fox Keller; feminist epistemology: for and against). *The Monist*, 77(4), 509–530.

Somma, M., & Tolleson-Rinehart, S. (1997, March). Tracking the elusive green women: Sex, environmentalism, and feminism in the United States and Europe. *Political Research Quarterly*, 50(1), 153.

Sonnert, G., with Holton, G. (1995). *Gender differences in science careers: The project access study*. New Brunswick, NJ: Rutgers University Press.

Soper, K. (1995). Feminism and ecology: Realism and rhetoric in the discourses of nature. *Science, Technology, & Human Values*, 20(3), 311–331.

Spallone, P. (1989). *Beyond conception: The new politics of reproduction.* Granby, MA: Bergin & Garvey.

Spallone, P., & Steinberg, D. L. (1987). *Made to order: The myth of reproductive and genetic progress.* New York: Pergamon Press.

Spanier, B. (1991). Gender and ideology in science: A study of molecular biology. *NWSA Journal, 3*(2), 167–198.

Spanier, B. (1995). Biological determinism and homosexuality. *NWSA Journal, 7*(1), 54–71.

Spanier, B. (1995). *Im/partial science: Gender ideology in molecular biology.* Bloomington: Indiana University Press.

Sperling, S. (1991, Autumn). Baboons with briefcases: Feminism, functionalism, and sociobiology in the evolution of primate gender. *Signs, 17*(1), 1–27.

Spitler, P. D. (1992, May–June). Reproductive religion. (Public opinion on motherhood). *The Humanist, 52*(3), 22–23.

Spretnak, C. (1993). Critical and constructive contributions of ecofeminism. *Bucknell Review, 37*(2), 181.

Squeezed out of science. (1992, February 3). *The Scientist, 6*(3), 1–1.

Squier, S. (1996, October). Fetal subjects and maternal objects: Reproductive technology and the new fetal/maternal relation. *Journal of Medicine and Philosophy, 21*(5), 515–536.

Stabile, C. A. (1994). *Feminism and the technological fix.* New York: Manchester University Press.

Stabile, C. A. (1994). "A garden inclosed is my sister": Ecofeminism and ecovalences. *Cultural Studies, 8*(1), 56.

Stamps, J. A. (1995, August). Sociobiology: Its evolution and intellectual descendents. *Politics and the Life Sciences,* pp. 191–193.

Stanworth, M. (Ed.). (1987). *Reproductive technologies: Gender, motherhood, and medicine.* Minneapolis: University of Minnesota Press.

Stark-Ademec, C. (1981, September/October). Women and science. *International Journal of Women's Studies, 4*(4), 311–338.

Starkey, P. (1998, Autumn). A rethink for women in science: Believes that current initiatives to encourage more women into science are missing the point. *Science and Public Affairs,* p. 5.

Staudt, K. A., & Jaquette, J. S. (1983). Women and development: Introduction. In *Women in developing countries: A policy focus* (pp. 1–6). New York: Haworth Press.

Stearney, L. M. (1994, Spring). Feminism, ecofeminism, and the maternal archetype: Motherhood as a feminine universal. *Communication Quarterly, 42*(2), 145.

Steinberg, D. L. (1994). Power, positionality and epistemology: Towards an antioppressive feminist standpoint approach to science, medicine and technology. *Women: A Cultural Review, 5*(3), 295–305.

Stepulevage, L., & Plumeridge, S. (1998). Women taking positions within computer science. *Gender and Education, 10*(3), 313.

Sterba, J. P. (Ed.). (1995). *Earth ethics: Environmental ethics, animal rights, and practical applications.* Englewood Cliffs, NJ: Prentice-Hall.

Stetson, D. M. (1996). Feminist perspectives on abortion and reproductive technologies. In M. Githens & D. M. Stetson (Eds.), *Abortion politics: Public policy in cross-cultural perspective* (pp. 211–223). New York: Routledge.

Stolcke, V. (1988). New reproductive technologies: The old quest for fatherhood. *Reproductive & Genetic Engineering, 1*(1), 5–20.

Stolte-Heiskanen, V., & First-Dilic, R. (Eds.). (1991). *Women in science: Token women or gender equality?* New York: St. Martin's Press.

Stone-Mediatore, S. (1998, Spring). Chandra Mohanty and the revaluing of "experience." [Special issue: Border crossings: Multicultural and postcolonial feminist challenges to philosophy, part 1]. *Hypatia, 13*(2), 116–133.

A strategy of sisterhood: Jaleh Daie, president of the Association for Women in Science and a professor of biology at the University of Wisconsin, Madison, proposes a strategic alliance of organizations supporting women's advancement in science and technology in order to ensure equitable representation of women at the national policymaking tables. (1997). *The Scientist, 11*(23), 8.

Stuart, B. H. (1996). People in physics, women in nuclear science. *Physics Education, 31*(2), 116.

Subrahmanyan, L. (1995). Patrifocality and the entry of women into science. *Higher Education, 30*(1), 1.

Suiter, M. (1991, January). Tomorrow's geoscientists: Recruiting and keeping them. *Geotimes, 36*(1), 12.

Suleri, S. (1992, Summer). Woman skin deep: Feminism and the postcolonial condition. (Identities). *Critical Inquiry, 18*(4), 756–769.

Summer, F. M., & Kerr, S. (1995). Making the links: Why bioregionalism needs ecofeminism. *Alternatives, 21*(2), 22.

Summer research program for undergraduate women and minorities. (1993, August 2). *Chemical and Engineering News, 71*(31), 31.

Summit held to find ways to attract women to science. (1994, October 5). *Chronicle of Higher Education, 41*(6), A19.

Sutherland, D. (1994, Winter). Speaking truth to power: Oppositional research practice and colonial power. *Resources for Feminist Research, 23*(4), 42–54.

Swedberg, L. (1993). Fallible or lovable: Response to Anne Fausto-Sterling's "Building two-way streets." *NWSA Journal, 5*(3), 389–391.

Tang-Martinez, Z. (1992). Women in science: Demanding a bigger piece of the pie or a new recipe? *Bulletin of Science, Technology & Society, 12*(4–5), 192–194.

Terry, J., & Calvert, M. (Eds.). (1997). *Processed lives: Gender and technology in everyday life.* New York: Routledge.

Terry, J. M., & Baird, W. E. (1997). What factors affect attitudes toward women in science held by high school biology students? *School Science and Mathematics, 97*(2), 78.

Theriot, N. M. (1993, August). Women's voices in nineteenth-century medical discourse: A step toward deconstructing science. *Signs, 19*(1), 1–31.

Tomaselli, S. (1991, June 1). Reflections on the history of the science of woman. *History of Science, 29*(84), 185–205.

Tong, R. (1997). *Feminist approaches to bioethics: Theoretical Reflections and practical applications*. Boulder, CO: Westview Press.

Tracy, K. B. (1998). From our readers: Women in science: The myth of "having it all." *Equity & Excellence in Education: University of Massachusetts School of Education Journal, 31*(2), 68.

Treichler, P. A., Cartwright, L., & Penley, C. (1998). *The visible woman: Imaging technologies, gender, and science*. New York: New York University Press.

Trigwell, K. (1990, January). The effects of an alternative science degree programme on the participation of women in the physical sciences. *International Journal of Science Education, 12*(1), 25–34.

Trimble, V. (1996). Commentary: Although science has become more gender-neutral and occasionally even favors female applicants, the status of women in science is still the subject of many complaints. *The Scientist, 10*(17), 11.

Tripp-Knowles, P. (1995, Spring). A review of the literature on barriers encountered by women in science academia. *Resources for Feminist Research, 24*(1/2), 28–34.

Tripp-Knowles, P. (1993). Margaret Benston's feminist science critique: A review and tribute. *Canadian Woman Studies/Les Cahiers de la Femme, 13*(2), 25–27.

Tripp-Knowles, P. (1994). Androcentric bias in science? *Women's Studies International Forum, 17*(1), 1–8.

Tuana, N. (Ed.). (1989). *Feminism and science*. Bloomington: Indiana University Press.

Tuana, N. (1993). *The less noble sex: Scientific, religious, and philosophical conceptions of woman's nature*. Bloomington: Indiana University Press.

Tuana, N. (1993, Spring). III [Comment on Anne Fausto-Sterling's "Building two-way streets"]. *NWSA Journal, 5*(1), 56–64.

Tuana, N. (1995). The values of science: Empiricism from a feminist perspective. *Synthese, 104*(3), 441–461.

Tuana, N. (1996). Revaluing science: Starting from the practices of women. *Synthese Library*, no. 256, 17.

U.S. agencies to fight for cash. Internet comes to the aid of women in science. (1996). *Nature, 382*(6590), 383.

Valente, M. (1998, March 27). Women who pursue a career in science or technology in Argentina face greater difficulties than their male counterparts and, as a result, remain a minority in the higher echelon. Available from Interpress Service.

Valverde, M., & Weir, L. (1997, Summer). Regulating new reproductive and genetic technologies: A feminist view of recent Canadian government initiatives. *Feminist Studies, 23*(2), 419–423.

Van Dijck, J. (1995). *Manufacturing babies and public consent: Debating the new reproductive technologies*. New York: New York University Press.

Vance, L. (1997, Fall). Ecofeminism and wilderness. *NWSA Journal, 9*(3), 60.

Wadsworth, E. M. (1992). Women's activities and women engineers: Expansions over time. *Initiatives, 55*(2), 59.

Wagner, I. (1994). Connecting communities of practice: Feminism, science, and technology. *Women's Studies International Forum, 17*(2–3), 257–265.

Wajcman, J. (1991). *Feminism confronts technology* Cambridge, MA: Polity Press.

Walker, M. (1998, Winter). Water notes: On women and science. *Canadian Woman Studies/Les Cahiers de la Femme, 17*(4), 113–114.

Warren, K. J., & Cheney, J. (1991, Spring). Ecological feminism and ecosystem ecology. *Hypatia, 6*(1), 179–197.

Warren, M. A. (1989, Fall). The moral significance of birth. *Hypatia, 4*(3), 46–65.

Wear, D. (1996). *Women in medical education: An anthology of experience.* New York: State University of New York Press.

Wear, D. (1997). *Privilege in the medical academy: A feminist examines gender, race, and power.* New York: Teachers College Press.

Weasel, L. (1997, January–February). The cell in relation: An ecofeminist revision of cell and molecular biology. *Women's Studies International Forum, 20*(1), 49–60.

Weisbard, P., & Apple, R. (Eds.). (1994). *The history of women and science, health, and technology: A bibliographic guide to the professions and the disciplines.* Madison: University of Wisconsin System Memorial Library.

Where are science's women? (1992, November 16). *Chemistry and Industry,* no. 22, 878.

Who's on the masthead? (1996). *The Scientist, 10*(5), 1.

Wijngaard, M. Van Den. (1992). Feminisme En biologisch Onderzoek Naar Seksev-erschillen [Feminism and biological research into sexual differences]. *Tidjschrift Voor Vrowenstudies, 13*(3), 354–369.

Wijngaard, M. Van Den. (1997). *Reinventing the sexes: The biomedical construction of femininity and masculinity.* Bloomington: Indiana University Press.

Wilkerson, A. L. (1998). *Diagnosis: The moral authority of medicine.* Ithaca, NY: Cornell University Press.

Wilkinson, S., & Kitzinger, C. (1994). *Women and health: Feminist perspectives.* Bristol, PA: Taylor & Francis.

Van Wingerden, I. (1993, July–August). "Once you have seen how scientific knowledge is made, you give up the idea that what you are 'discovering' may actually be 'nature.'" *Women's Studies International Forum, 16*(4), 379–380.

Wismer, S. (1998, Winter). Eighteen tips: A guide for including everybody in science, technology, engineering and mathematics. *Canadian Woman Studies/ Les Cahiers de la Femme, 17*(4), 115–118.

Witt, P. L., Bauerle, C., Derouen, D., Kamel, D., Kelleher, P., Mccarthy, M., Namenwirth, M., Sabatini, L., & Voytovich, M. (1989). The October 29th group: Defining a feminist science. *Women's Studies International Forum, 12*(3), 253–259.

Wolf, S. M. (1996). *Feminism & bioethics: Beyond reproduction.* New York: Oxford University Press.

Women heroes of science: A bibliography: A selection of titles about the history of women in science. (1991, March 1). *Science Books & Films, 27*(2), 33–34.

Women in science. (1995). *Geotimes, 40*(11), 55.

Women in science. (1996). *Materials World: The Journal of the Institute of Materials, 4*(9), 508.

Women in science. (1998). *Chemical and Engineering News, 76*(11), 11.

Women in science. (1998). *The Scientist, 12*(8), 1.

Women in science: Beyond the false summit. (1996). *ASM News, 62*(3), 120.

Women in science '93: Gender and the culture of science. (1993, April 6). *Science, 260*(5106), 383.

Women in science: A report of committee W. (1996). *Academe: Bulletin of the AAUP, 82*(3), 57.

Women in science: U.K. panel floats a plan. (1994, March 4). *Science, 263*(5151), 1215.

Women in science—Why so few? (1994, October). *Scientific, Engineering, Technical Manpower Comments, 31*(7), 20.

Women in science & engineering. (1994, September). *Scientific, Engineering, Technical Manpower Comments, 31*(6), 18.

Women scientists: Conference marks progress of women in science and engineering over past 25 years. (1998). *Chemical and Engineering News, 76*(14), 37.

Women stay out of science: A number of organisations are trying to lure more of the soaring number of women higher education students into science and technology. (1994). *Labour Research, 83*(4), 19.

Women's groups and scientists face-to-face in Geneva meeting. (1993, Spring). *Vitality, 15*(1), 8–9.

Woodhouse, H. (1997). Tradition or modernity? The fallacy of misplaced concreteness among women science educators in Cameroon. *Interchange, 28*(2–3), 253.

Worell, J., & Etaugh, C. (1994, December). Transforming theory and research with women: Themes and variation. *Psychology of Women Quarterly, 18*(4), 443–450.

Wright, J. (1995, May). Encouraging young women to study science: A Nebraska success. *ACSM Bulletin*, no. 155, 17.

Wright, M. (1998, Summer). "Maquiladora mestizas" and a feminist border politics: Revisiting Anzaldua. [Special issue: Border crossings: Multicultural and postcolonial feminist challenges to philosophy, part 2]. *Hypatia, 13*(3), 114–131.

Wygoda, L. J. (1993, November).Women in science. *The Science Teacher, 60*(8), 24.

Wylie, A., Okruhlik, K., Thielen-Wilson, L., & Morton, S. (1989). Feminist critiques of science: The feminist epistemological and methodological literature. *Women's Studies International Forum, 12*(3), 379–388.

Wylie, A., Okruhlik, K., Thielen-Wilson, L., & Morton, S. (1990). Philosophical feminism: A bibliographic guide to critiques of science. *Resources for Feminist Research/Documentation sur la Recherche Feministe, 19*(2), 2–38.

Wymelenberg, S. (1990). *Science and babies: Private decisions, public dilemmas.* Washington, DC: National Academy Press.

Yarrison-Rice, J. M. (1995). On the problem of making science attractive for women and minorities: An annotated bibliography. *American Journal of Physics, 63*(3), 203.

Yee, C. Z. (1977, Fall). Women in science and technology need the women's movement? *Frontiers, 2*(3), 125–128.

Yuval-Davis, N. (1996, January–April). Women and the biological reproduction of "The Nation." *Women's Studies International Forum, 19*(1–2), 17–24.

Zimmermann, P. R. (1993, April–June). The female bodywars: Rethinking feminist media politics. *Socialist Review, 23*(2), 35–59.

Zita, J. N. (1988, Spring). The feminist question of the science question in feminism. *Hypatia, 3*, 157–168.

Zorilla, S. F., Dides, C. C., Hevia, A. L., & Munita, G. A. (1997, April–June). The concerns of bioethics. *Women's Health Journal*, no. 2, 38–40.

Zuk, M. (1993, December). Feminism and the study of animal behavior. *Bioscience, 43*(11), 774–778.

Zumdahl, S. A. (1996, Fall). Mission impossible? Improving retention of science majors among minorities and women. *Journal of Chemical Education, 73*(11), A26.

Index

About the Author

Sue V. Rosser received her Ph.D. in Zoology from the University of Wisconsin at Madison in 1973. Since July 1999, she has served as Dean of the Ivan Allen College at Georgia Institute of Technology in Atlanta, where she is also Professor of History, Technology, and Society. From 1995 to 1999, she was Director of the Center for Women's Studies and Gender Research and Professor of Anthropology at the University of Florida. During 1994–95, she served as Senior Program Officer for Women's Programs at the National Science Foundation, while on leave from her position as Director of Women's Studies for the University of South Carolina System and Professor of Family and Preventive Medicine.

Author of more than 85 journal articles on theoretical and applied issues surrounding women and science and women's health, she has written seven previous books: *Teaching Science and Health from a Feminist Perspective* (1986), *Feminism within the Science and Health Care Professions* (1988), *Female Friendly Science* (1990), *Biology & Feminism* (1992), *Women's Health: Missing from U.S. Medicine* (1994), *Teaching the Majority* (1995), and *Re-engineering Female Friendly Science* (1997). Recipient of several NSF grants, during 1993 she was Visiting Distinguished Professor for Women and Science in the University of Wisconsin System.